CW01011328

CONTENTS

Chapter 1

Origins and Development of the Panzergrenadier

6

Chapter 2

Panzergrenadier Organisation and Tactics

18

Chapter 3

Panzergrenadiers in Action in the West, 1939–45

30

Chapter 4

Panzergrenadiers in Action on the Eastern Front, 1941–45

44

Chapter 5

The Firepower of a Panzergrenadier

60

Chapter 6

Mobility for the Panzergrenadier

76

Appendix

93

Index

95

Origins and Development of the Panzergrenadier

After the bloody carnage of World War I, generals and tacticians of all sides sought a means of ensuring that such slaughter would not happen again. The new German theory of *blitzkrieg*, or 'lightning war', required an infantryman who could keep pace with the tanks – the panzergrenadier was born.

FEW WOULD ARGUE that the key to Germany's brilliant campaigns of the first years of World War II was the German Army's bold and innovative use of the tank. However, Heinz Guderian, the father of the German panzer arm, realised that the tank was rarely effective when operating alone and needed the close support of artillery and particularly infantry to achieve success. The problem was how to give the infantry a level of mobility similar to the tanks so they could be deployed quickly when required. The answer was to provide the infantry with motorised transport, initially lorries, but later, armoured personnel carriers, usually the famous Sd Kfz 251 half track. These motorised infantry who accompanied the panzers into battle were known as panzergrenadiers in the German Army. The key to the success of the panzers was the effective and self-contained mix of forces: artillery, engineers, anti-aircraft batteries and infantry. The panzer forces had their panzergrenadiers and thus did not have to wait for the mass of ordinary infantry divisions to catch up on foot or by rail. Breakthroughs could be rapidly exploited because the panzergrenadiers fought at the pace of the tank. They were a vital and integral component of the fearsome German panzer arm and without question can be placed among the elite formations of World War II.

WORLD WAR I

Despite the technological advances of the late nineteenth and early twentieth centuries, such as rapid-firing artillery, the magazine loading rifle, barbed wire and the machine-gun, all the armies of the major combatants entered World War I with substantial numbers of cavalry amongst their forces. The Germans had 11 cavalry divisions, the French 10, the Russians 36, the Austrians 11, the British two and the Belgians one. These 335,000 mounted men were, as British military historians Richard Holmes and John Keegan point out, considerably more than the number with which Genghis Khan subdued most of Eurasia in the thirteenth century. A century, perhaps a century and a half, of military experience had pointed to the vulnerability of mounted men in modern warfare, yet this was ignored almost uniformly by the European military. The 1909 German field regulations stated that: 'Mounted action is still the predominant way in which cavalry fights.'

That very year, however, General Alfred Graf von Schlieffen, who as the Chief of the German General Staff had devised the plan for attacking France through Belgium, had baldly proclaimed that in his view of the current battlefield: 'Not a horseman will be seen. The cavalry will have to accomplish its tasks out of the range of the infantry and artillery. Breech-loaders and machine guns will have banished the cavalry quite mercilessly from the battlefield.' In

Left: German stormtroopers advancing on the Aisne during the Ludendorff offensives of early 1918. For maximum mobile fire-power, these stormtroopers are carrying the MG 08/15, which weighed a hefty 18kg (39.7lbs).

During an advance, panzergrenadiers accompanying the tanks in armoured personnel carriers would be expected to deploy at a moment's notice to 'mop up' any remaining enemy pockets of resistance.

the opening battles of World War I five years later, it was von Schlieffen, not his army's field regulations, who was proved right. Whenever cavalry met well-formed infantry they were shot from their horses in droves. Within six weeks the horse was banished from the Western European battlefield. Nonetheless, all High Commands – often populated by cavalry officers – hankered after using them to exploit the elusive breakthrough. Even in 1916, at the Battle of the Somme, the British had three cavalry divisions ready to pour through the gaps that the infantry (and a few early tanks) never managed to punch through the German lines. Although cavalry remained useful in the East and in subsidiary theatres such as the Middle East, it would never again play an important role. A key element of strategic and tactical mobility was removed forever from the battlefield.

What von Schlieffen had not forecast was that the infantry would be as vulnerable as the cavalry to the developments in weaponry. The emphasis placed by Europe's armies upon

the charge and bayonet was as misplaced as the belief in the efficacy of cavalry. The outnumbered British, French and Belgians fought to a standstill what was considered by some 'the finest army in the world' at terrible cost to themselves. The firepower that had shattered the cavalry charges proceeded to do the same to the bayonet charges of the following weeks. The exhausted armies dug in and the war settled into stalemate, the trenches of both sides stretching from the Alps to the North Sea.

The Struggle to Break the Stalemate

Initially the generals turned to artillery to break the deadlock. The tactic was simple: assemble artillery pieces, lots of them, pulverise the enemy's trenches, possibly for days on end, and then send the infantry over to pick up the pieces. Unfortunately there were usually enough of the well-dug-in defenders, or enough men in reserve, to repulse an attack or recapture any ground lost by immediate counter-attack. Yet the high commands persevered through the slaughter

Right: Heinz Guderian in his command half-track directing operations during the invasion of France in 1940. The operators in the foreground are working an ENIGMA cipher machine, a coding device that the Allies managed to break early in the war.

Above: British troops advancing behind an early Mark 1 Male tank, 1916. The wheels at the tank's rear are an early steering device, discarded on later models. The first British tanks were deployed in penny packets and achieved little.

of Vosges, Lorraine and Neuve Chapelle in 1915; Lozono, Verdun and the Somme in 1916; Arras, Chemin des Dames, and Ypres in 1917, at the cost of hundreds of thousands of their men's lives. There were attempts at innovation with the use of new weapons, such as poison gas, but none had proved decisive. The Battle of the Somme provides a suitable example of the terrible vulnerability of human beings on the modern battlefield, and the fact that the machine-gun had reduced mobility to almost nothing. Despite a seven day preceding bombardment, the attacking British troops sustained some 60,000 casualties – perhaps 30,000 in the first hour – on the opening day of the battle. Over the four months of the Somme offensive, after an effort unequalled in British military history and the loss of over 400,000 men, British troops advanced no further than ten miles. Amongst the slaughter of the Somme, however, the British did introduce a new weapon, the tank.

The Arrival of the Tank

The British had spent most of 1915 and the first half of 1916 developing a tracked armoured fighting vehicle capable of traversing trenches and overcoming barbed wire. The first 100 ordered by the British Army were referred to as 'water tanks' for security reasons and the name stuck. The driving force behind the programme, Colonel E. D. Swinton, had specific ideas as to how the new weapon should be used. Heinz Guderian considered Swinton's ideas so sound he quoted them at length and noted that: 'It was fortunate for the Germans that from the outset the British shrank from following these guidelines.' Swinton rejected the traditional

'step-by-step' limited offensive but rather advocated using tanks as part of 'a violent effort ... to burst right through the enemy's defensive zone in one great rush.' He continued:

'Not only, however, does it seem that the tanks will confer the power to force successive comparatively unbattered defensive lines, but as has been explained, the more speedy and uninterrupted their advance the greater the chance of their surviving sufficiently long to do this. It is possible, therefore, that an effort to break right through the enemy's defensive zone in one day may now be contemplated as a feasible operation.'

This was not far from Guderian's own theories which he developed in the inter-war years. Swinton was determined that the tank 'should not be used in driblets ... but in one great combined operation'. The British commander, General Sir Douglas Haig, proceeded to do exactly the opposite and deploy a handful of tanks to prop up the Somme offensive. Swinton protested and was promptly sacked by Haig. The 32 tanks deployed on 15 September 1916 achieved little beyond a few local successes. There was no big breakthrough.

When tanks were concentrated and used properly things could be different. On 20 November 1917, near the village of Cambrai, 381 tanks, some radio equipped, were concentrated on a six-mile frontage. There was no preliminary barrage which had announced previous British tank attacks and thus the ground was not a morass of craters. The tanks achieved complete surprise, punching four miles through the German lines. The British captured 7500 prisoners at minimal cost. It was a stunning success and church bells in Britain were rung to celebrate the victory. This was premature, for the momentum of the attack was not maintained. The Germans soon counter-attacked and regained what they had lost.

Although Cambrai showed the potential of tanks when properly used, the failures of the battle were also instructive.

The lack of progress made by the British at the centre of the attack had grave consequences for the advance and illustrated the need for close cooperation between tanks and their supporting infantry. The 51st (Highland) Division was held up by stiff German resistance in contrast to the formations around them. The Division's commander, Major-General Harper, had no experience of working with tanks and believed they would draw fire on his men. He therefore ordered his men to keep well behind the advancing tanks in contradiction to the agreed plan. The German artillery was able to knock the tanks out with relative ease, and once the infantry advanced, the German machine-gunners were able to halt the Highlanders as had happened so many times before. The need for proper infantry support was made extremely clear. Infantry could not advance without tanks across no-mans land and, as Guderian recognised later in his analysis of the battle: 'conversely unsupported armour cannot always be guaranteed to wipe out defending infantry'.

Early German Failures

The Germans had neither the technical knowledge nor the industrial capacity to produce enough tanks to use them in any quantity in World War I. The one German model to see service, the A7V – only 20 of which were built – was vastly inferior to British and French models. When the German commander, General Erich Ludendorff, launched his massive offensive in the spring of 1918, intended to knock the British and French out of the war before American troops arrived in any great numbers, he was forced to rely on artillery and infantry. However, the Ludendorff offensive demonstrated that the Germans had also applied some thought to the problem of breaking the stalemate. The German artillery had learnt to fire a brief preparatory barrage which neutralised the defence – particularly the enemy's communications systems – at the moment of assault. The leading German infantry formations – specially trained *stoss* (assault or storm) troops – infiltrated as quickly as possible into the depth of the enemy's defences, bypassing centres of resistance which would be overcome later by following troops. The combination of neutralisation and infiltration proved very successful and the Germans made considerable advances but were never able to fully exploit their penetrations and allowed the Allies to retreat in reasonable order. For a time the British and French

were in serious trouble, but the Germans also suffered massive loses. Therefore, when the British and French armies stiffened and Ludendorff's offensive failed to win the war, the German army was left in a much weakened state.

It was now that the German failure to develop their own sizable tank forces or decent anti-tank defences told against them. By 1918 the British and French had built up large tank forces and, as the German offensive petered out, they counter-attacked with the tank as their spearhead. On 8 August 1918, this force delivered a decisive stroke at the Battle of Amiens. The British, with 604 tanks, mostly the improved Mark V but also a number of the light Whippets capable of speeds of 8 mph, and the French, with 110 vehicles, accompanied by supporting infantry, broke through the German lines in the Somme salient in a single day to reach the open country beyond. Ludendorff later called it the 'Black Day for the German Army'. The Allied tanks – British, French and increasingly American – led the next three months of continuous advance until the Germans surrendered in November 1918.

The panzergrenadier was born from the experiences of 1914 to 1918. To understand his role in World War II, it is necessary to examine the tactical and technical developments of World War I. The most important and revolutionary innovation was the tank. Granted the submarine and aeroplane would dominate their elements and later play key

Below: German stormtroopers in action, somewhere on the Western Front. Stormtrooper tactics revolutionised small unit combat – men were encouraged to use stealthy means to approach the enemy, and carried a lot of firepower.

strategic roles, but the sea and the sky are essentially ancillary to land in warfare – particularly in the case of Germany – and in land operations following World War I the tank was to reign supreme. World War I had proved that cavalry no longer had any major role in modern warfare. Yet the cavalry had traditionally provided the mobility that generals had always sought. The tank had restored a degree of mobility to the battlefield and that mobility could only increase. Indeed, by 1918 the British were working on vehicles that could reach 30 mph and Colonel J.F.C. Fuller had drawn up the imaginative 'Plan 1919' whereby these fast new tanks, supported by aircraft, would penetrate the German lines and attack the headquarters and communication centres of the enemy leadership. Deprived of its 'brain', Fuller reckoned that the front would collapse in 'a matter of hours'. The tank had also allowed Allied infantry to move on the battlefield once again, although Ludendorff's offensive and the new German 'storm trooper' tactics had proved that infantry, used imaginatively, were still an effective offensive arm. Those with foresight, such as Fuller, saw these two developments in combination as extremely potent. What battlefield experience had truly illustrated, however, was the interdependence of the two arms: tanks allowed the infantry

to re-emerge from their trenches, but conversely the tank was extremely vulnerable without infantry support. The real problem was to devise a method of utilising the shock effect of the tank with its prospective increase in speed and mobility while allowing the infantry to keep up and thus ensure that unsupported tanks were not knocked out with comparative ease by the defenders.

THE DEVELOPMENTS OF THE INTER-WAR YEARS

Despite the rapid advances in tank technology and tactics in the last years of World War I, the weapon rapidly faded from its pre-eminent wartime position. A remark by a British officer to J.F.C. Fuller on the day after the war ended in 1918 is indicative: 'Thank God we can now get back to real soldiering'. 'Real soldiering' had little room for the tank within the traditional military hierarchy where combat functions centred around infantry, artillery and cavalry. Tanks held a low position in this order of things, if they held a place at all. With Germany banned from possessing tanks under the peace settlement and the Soviet Union bankrupted and exhausted by revolution and civil war, opportunities

How to use an entrenching tool as a weapon: a demonstration of training for hand-to-hand combat.

As shown here, panzergrenadiers were trained to fight with their entrenching tools: an effective weapon at close range.

Above: A German motorised unit arranged for inspection during the inter-war years, a typical example of motorised troops at this time. The Germans relied heavily on motorcycles and soft-skinned vehicles before (and during) the war.

for developing armoured forces remained solely with the victorious democracies. The United States Army, for example, had established a tank corps in 1918. The corps was abolished in 1920 and its tanks assigned to the infantry.

The French did not do much better. They also assigned their tanks to the infantry in 1920. To an extent this reflected the French experience of World War I. Early use of tanks, such as at the battle at Chemins des Dames in October 1917, convinced the French Command that only when tanks operated in close coordination with the infantry were they successful. This was correct so far as it went, when applied to the wartime conditions of the Western Front. Nonetheless, the French had relegated the tank to the role of an infantry support weapon, and the speed of their advance would be limited to that of the infantry on foot. This did not matter too much when the enemy did not have effective anti-tank weapons – as was the case with the Germans at Chemins des Dames – nor when tanks could not reach speeds much higher than walking pace anyway. Tanks were deployed with each line of advancing infantry. However, as Guderian pointed out : 'the practice of subordinating tanks to ... infantry also frustrated any attempt to exploit the success of the first wave of armour in a speedy and energetic way'. This fault notwithstanding, such ponderous use of tanks was similarly dismissed by the German with the remark: 'In future such tactics will be suicidal'. Yet as he also noted in 1937 these tactics had 'remained a fundamental tenet of French tank tactics until the present day'.

The French tanks were spread among their infantry divisions and indicative of this was the change in nomenclature for French tanks in the 1930s when 'assault tanks' were renamed 'accompanying tanks'. Colonel Charles de Gaulle advocated in his 1933 work, *Vers l'Armée de Métier* (Towards a Professional Army) that the French Army form a mobile armoured force, but he had no new ideas of how to use it. Nonetheless, France formed the world's first armoured division, the *division légère mécanique* (light mechanised division) in 1934, although it was too 'light' in tanks to be much use in combat. By 1940 they also had three heavy armoured divisions equipped with probably the best tanks in Europe at the time, the Char B1 *bis* and the Somua S35. Where the French failed hopelessly was in the way they used their tanks. Fighting at the pace of the infantry and deploying their tanks in penny packets or spreading them thinly as a forward reconnaissance screen, they were disastrously defeated when the Germans invaded.

Fuller, Liddell Hart and the Experimental Mechanised Force

By far the most innovative work on armoured warfare was undertaken by the British in the first decade or so after the end of World War I. Considering its shrinking size and budgets, the pioneering efforts of the Royal Tank Corps are quite remarkable. The Experimental Mechanised Force was established in 1927. Between 1927 and 1931 this force, despite numerous handicaps, conducted a series of ground-breaking manoeuvres and trials, with increasingly high levels of mechanisation and coordination by radio. However, some sections of the Tank Corps became increasingly tank centred and played down the importance of other arms as they experienced problems with lorried infantry and towed artillery. To quote Colonel Eric Offord: 'We didn't want an all tank army but what could we do? The infantry were in buses [i.e. trucks], they couldn't come with us. The artillery were...obstructive. They never put the rounds where you needed them; and when you called it always came too late.' The British tank men were more and more inclined to operate tanks on their own, with little regard to infantry and artillery cooperation. This inclination was to cause the British considerable problems in the Western Desert a few years later. Nonetheless, the British were leaders in mechanised warfare, but it was a lead soon squandered as lack of finance

and traditionalist opposition led to other parts of the army receiving more funds.

At the same time, Britain also produced some of the most interesting writing on mechanisation – Fuller and Basil Liddell Hart being merely the most famous theorists. Fuller, author of 'Plan 1919', was an out-and-out advocate of full mechanisation and the importance of tanks for the army. He wrote widely on the future role of armoured forces. Liddell Hart was much influenced by the German tactics of 1918 when he rewrote the British infantry training manual directly after the war. After retiring due to ill health, he continued to promote the idea of full mechanisation and highly mobile mixed tank and motorised infantry units as a way of avoiding the slaughter of World War I. Liddell Hart built upon Fuller's tactical ideas concerning penetrating the enemy's line, and striking at his headquarters with his philosophy of 'expanding torrents' which could be applied at the strategic level, the so-called 'indirect approach'. Guderian was familiar with their work and acknowledges a considerable debt to them in his 1952 work *Panzer Leader*, where he noted that: 'Deeply impressed by these ideas I tried to develop then in a sense practicable for our own army.'

Below: Panzer Mark 1 tanks on display manoeuvres at a Nuremburg rally in 1938. After seeing these tanks being demonstrated for the first time, Hitler exclaimed: 'That's what I need. That's what I want to have.'

Heinz Guderian, the Panzers and Motorised Infantry

There were numerous lessons to be learnt from World War I and the inter-war years. The war had illustrated the vulnerability of unsupported tanks and the dangers of deploying tanks in penny packets. The French decided to use their tanks in a subordinate role to the supporting infantry. The British tank men grew disillusioned with cooperation with other arms and were inclined to believe tanks could operate independently. Meanwhile, the British military authorities were inclined to spend their meagre peacetime budget elsewhere. Only in Germany were the correct conclusions about mechanisation – particularly tank–infantry cooperation – drawn, and the key exponent was Heinz Guderian.

Under the terms of the World War I peace settlement signed at Versailles in June 1919, Germany was forbidden the possession of important weapon systems such as aircraft, U-boats and heavy artillery. The German Army was restricted to 100,000 men. Crucially, the possession, purchase or development of tanks was forbidden. Although the small size of the German Army rankled with the German military, the chief of the German staff, General Hans von Seekt, was determined that the *Reichswehr*, as the German armed forces were now called, be as potent a military force as its size allowed. Its small size also allowed concentration on quality in both training and military techniques. There is no doubt that von Seekt intended the *Reichswehr* to provide a cadre for a future expansion of the German Army.

Eager to support new military ideas, von Seekt gave considerable backing to Germany's leading tank enthusiast Heinz Guderian. Guderian had spent the early part of the 1920s studying the works of British armoured warfare theorists such as Liddell Hart and J.F.C. Fuller. While working at the Inspectorate of Motorised Troops, Guderian tried to apply their theories to the German Army. In 1924 he suggested transforming the motorised units of the supply troops he commanded into combat formations. He was told by his superior von Natzmer: 'To hell with combat, they are supposed to carry flour.' However, von Seekt was supportive and a core of German senior officers began to take seriously the possibility of conducting mobile warfare based around armoured vehicles. In about 1925, a limited programme of training and close cooperation began, and the following year the Germans held full-scale manoeuvres with mechanised forces. These exercises were hampered by a complete lack of tanks and other types of armoured vehicles, all still forbidden under the Treaty of Versailles. In the place of tanks, soldiers had to carry cardboard tank silhouettes. By 1928 the Germans

Above: The stereotypical image of the panzergrenadiers – an armoured halftrack (Sd Kfz 251) on the Eastern Front, loaded with troops. In reality, panzergrenadiers often went into combat in soft-skinned lorries, or even walked.

had progressed to using 'motorised dummies of sheet metal'. As Guderian himself noted, despite his theorising and preoccupation, he was 'totally lacking in all practical experience of tanks...I had never even seen inside of one'.

There was no question of direct access to Western design, so the Germans turned to the Soviet Union in an effort to experiment with tank design away from the prying eyes of Britain and France. In 1926 the Germans established a tank school at Kazan, deep in the Soviet Union, and here Germany's first post-war tanks were built. Most were little more than one-off experiments, but Guderian, who by 1932 was a lieutenant colonel and chief of staff at the Inspectorate of Motorised Troops, and Captain Pirner, responsible for tank production, had worked out a programme of equipment for tank or panzer divisions that Guderian was eager to establish. In the meantime, they agreed on the building of a stop-gap light tank based on the Carden Lloyd tankette, designated the Pz Kpfw I. Hitler, who came to power in 1933, gave the Panzer Pz Kpfw I his backing, remarking: 'That's what I need. That's what I want to have.' For Guderian, this cheap and simple vehicle was perfect for training and experimental manoeuvres.

Hitler cheerfully disregarded the restrictions of Versailles and a massive expansion programme of the German armed forces took place. Using his light tanks, the Pz Kpfw I and later the Pz Kpfw II, Guderian could develop his theories of armoured warfare through practical experience on exercises. He was unique amongst armoured warfare theorists in the

1920s due to the support he received from his superiors and his government. Admittedly, Marshal Tukhachevsky had trained and equipped large armoured formations in the Soviet Union, but he and his theories disappeared during Stalin's purge of the Red Army in the late 1930s. In 1935, the French formed the world's first armoured division. In response, the Germans formed three. There were not really enough tanks or vehicles available to equip these formations. Nonetheless, Guderian had by 1937 enough experience of operating these forces to put his theories of armoured warfare in writing in his seminal work *Achtung – Panzer!*

Guderian's Ideas

Guderian argued that it was ridiculous to waste the speed and mobility of the tank by tying it to the pace of the infantry. The tank had to be concentrated in a formation that could both punch through the enemy line and exploit the breakthrough

A schematic representation of the German *blitzkrieg* tactics: enemy forces are surrounded and bombarded from all sides, while the panzer forces push quickly on, leaving the panzergrenadiers to deal with any remaining threats.

by rapid advance. Unlike many contemporaries, Guderian did not argue that tanks could achieve this on their own. Armoured formations had to be large and include other supporting arms, such as artillery, engineers and infantry. The German panzer division combined these separate arms effectively for the first time and included a proportion of motorised infantry. As Guderian noted: 'This works best and most consistently when a certain number of infantry units are incorporated permanently with the tank units in a larger formation.'

In World War II, all panzer divisions contained a sizable motorised infantry, or panzergrenadier, component. In *Achtung – Panzer!* Guderian laid out their role in the fast moving armoured warfare he intended to undertake. Before a tank attack opened, he expected the infantry to support the armour and exploit any success. Thus, heavy infantry weapons would be ready to suppress anti-tank defences and any such areas bypassed by the tanks, whilst infantry would exploit any breakthrough by means of an immediate advance. As Guderian said: 'The infantry should be under no illusions: the tanks can cripple the enemy and knock a hole in their defensive system, but they cannot dispense with the need for infantry combat.' The infantry would then deal with any pockets of enemy resistance left behind by the tanks.

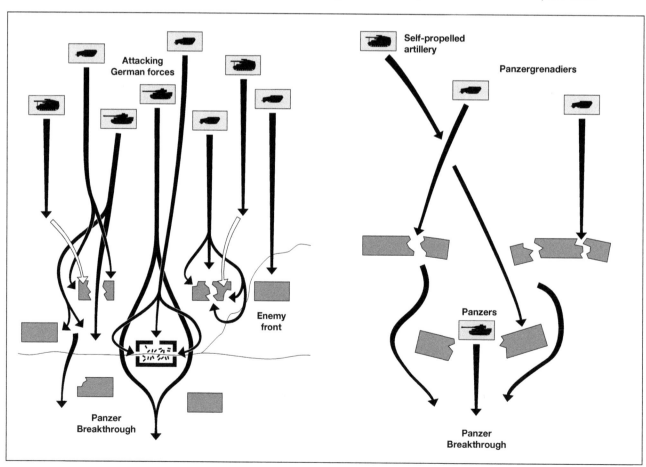

Infantry–Tank Cooperation

While he expected the tanks to lead any advance over favourable terrain, Guderian accepted that the infantry might need to attack ahead of the tanks should the latter encounter terrain such as rivers, built-up areas, fortified positions or minefields. Guderian accepted that accompanying a successful tank attack was a taxing business for the infantry, particularly if they were on foot. Yet 'the main tasks of supporting infantry are to follow up behind the tank attacks and complete their successes without delay'. The most effective way of doing this is with motorised infantry, 'especially' as Guderian believed: 'If the soldiers' vehicles have complete cross-country mobility... If such rifle units were united permanently with tanks in a single formation, it would form a comradeship in arms and at times of peace – a comradeship that would prove its worth when we come to seek a decision in the field. The benefits in terms of morale would be at least as great as the tactical ones.'

The German Army, however, was in no position in 1937, or even by the outbreak of war in 1939, to equip its motorised infantry units with armoured transport. Its motorised troops remained dependent upon unarmoured means of transport. Guderian summed up the situation thus:

'We do not possess armoured cross-country vehicles for transportation. Those of our infantry units that are destined for co-operation with tanks are therefore moved partly by motor-cycles and partly on cross-country trucks. The motor-cycle infantry have already performed well on reconnaissance in association with armoured reconnaissance vehicles, and they can be used for a whole variety of functions, since they are speedy, easy to conceal, and can make their way along any kind of road and across any terrain that is not altogether too difficult. We have plenty of good motorcycles in Germany and replacements present no problem. The

Above: Heavily-laden panzergrenadiers march into battle alongside a Pz Kpfw III tank during the advance into Russia. At this stage of the war, panzergrenadiers tended to walk rather than ride on the tanks in the Soviet fashion.

truck-borne infantry are protected against the elements, and in addition to the men and their equipment the vehicles carry extra loads such as ammunition, entrenching tools and engineering requisites, together with rations for several days. The present trucks are too bulky to be ideal; they have difficulty in negotiating narrow roads with sharp bends, and they are hard to conceal.'

Guderian was promoted to lieutenant general in 1938 and given command of the world's first armoured corps, overtaking several officers senior to him. He was given command of the spearhead of the German force that annexed Austria in the so-called *Anschluss* that same year. It was an opportunity to demonstrate his armoured units, given resistance to the union could not be entirely discounted. The *Anschluss* was a political success but a military failure. Guderian's armoured corps fared badly. Although the troops were greeted by cheering crowds, it highlighted all the logistical problems of armoured formations. Mechanical failures ran considerably higher than the 30 per cent admitted by the Germans. Tanks broke down and ran out of fuel, and Guderian was forced to threaten violence in order to use a fuel depot.

Guderian sought to improve the logistical failings of his divisions before war began in 1939. However, the armoured personnel carriers he desired for the motorised infantry within his panzer divisions were not available in any number by the time of the Polish campaign. The prototype panzergrenadiers fought and travelled in transport like that described by Guderian in 1937.

CHAPTER 2

Panzergrenadier Organisation and Tactics

Right from their early days as motorised infantry, the panzergrenadier divisions endured constant development and restructuring; first as new equipment emerged, and then later, as the tide of the war began to turn against Germany, as defence of the Reich became the priority.

THE TERM PANZERGRENADIER, when used uniformly for German motorised infantry during World War II, is somewhat imprecise. Firstly, the term panzergrenadier was not used in German nomenclature before June 1942 when the motorised infantry regiments known as *schützen* were renamed panzergrenadier regiments. All panzer divisions contained one or two regiments of *schützen*/panzergrenadiers. Actual panzergrenadier divisions were not formed until 1943. Nonetheless, their basis was the old motorised infantry divisions, some of which had been in existence from August 1939. Even then, a number of the panzergrenadier divisions subsequently converted to panzer divisions later in the war. It is safe to say that the motorised infantryman in a panzer or motorised infantry division was exactly the same type of soldier and undertook the same type of combat roles as his panzergrenadier successor in 1943–45.

Panzer and Motorised Infantry Divisions

The division is traditionally the smallest military formation in which all arms are combined. This used to be infantry, artillery and cavalry, but by the 1930s the cavalry had been replaced by tanks. These elements were placed under one

---

Left: Motorised infantry scan the horizon for opposition during the invasion of Poland. These troops would debus prior to contact with the enemy, as they were highly vulnerable to enemy fire in soft-skinned vehicles such as the one shown here.

command and were capable of fighting independently. The panzer division was even more complex. When the first three armoured divisions were formed in Germany in 1935, the ideal balance between tank and infantry had not yet been found. The offensive power of the new divisions rested firmly in its tank regiments, which possessed a total of some 560 tanks. The motorised infantry were originally regarded as very much a subsidiary arm, consisting of a single brigade made up of a single two-battalion rifle regiment and a motorcycle battalion. However, experimental manoeuvres showed that this was a poor balance between tanks and motorised infantry, and the rifle regiment was given an extra two battalions. The subsequent panzer divisions to be raised, prior to the invasion of Poland, were each given a couple of two-battalion rifle regiments, which became standard for all armoured formations. The number of tanks allocated actually decreased. By August 1939, one panzer company had been removed from each tank regiment and the number of tanks in a division had dropped to 328. If we take as an example the 1st Panzer Division that went to war on 1 September 1939 in Poland, we find as its motorised infantry complement the 1st *Schützen* Brigade, containing the 1st *Schützen* Regiment. This was divided into two motorised battalions, each of which contained a motorcycle company, two rifle companies and a heavy company containing the engineers, the infantry gun section and the anti-tank platoon. The brigade was completed by the second motorcycle battalion, which was made up of three

Panzergrenadier firing a Gewehr 98k rifle, the standard service rifle for all German soldiers during World War II. This artwork depicts a soldier late in the war – for example, he no longer wears the expensive knee-length jackboot.

Inset: An illustration from the German Army manual, instructing soldiers not to run away and risk being shot in the back when being attacked by tanks, but to remain in their foxholes and shoot at the accompanying infantry.

motorcycle companies, a motorcycle heavy machine-gun company and a heavy company, which provided support. As can be seen from the inventory, the motorised infantry relied on trucks and a very large number of motorcycles to provide their mobility.

In 1939, the motorised infantry division was a somewhat different concept. It had no integral armour itself, and usually one motorised division was attached to

two panzer divisions in a corps to provide extra mobile infantry support. The 2nd Motorised Infantry Division which fought in Poland was made up of three motorised infantry regiments. These contained three battalions made up of three rifle companies, a heavy company, *panzerabwehr* (anti-tank) company and an infantry support gun company. The division also had, within its artillery regiment, four battalions equipped with 105mm leFH and 150mm sFH guns. It also had a special anti-tank battalion, a reconnaissance battalion equipped with motorcycles and armoured cars, a pioneer battalion, a signals battalion and numerous supporting troops. Like their brethren in the panzer division, these motorised infantry continued to rely on trucks and motorcycles for their transport.

After the campaign in Poland, the four-battalion infantry regiment structure of the motorised divisions was changed. A leaner structure resulted in the deletion of one battalion, as four had proved too unwieldy in combat.

Nonetheless, the German High Command judged the four motorised divisions which saw service in Poland a considerable success, and thus nine more were formed by 1941 – although three of these belonged to the SS. By the time of the French campaign, the Sd Kfz 251 half-track was beginning to appear in the panzer divisions' *schützen* formations. Even so, they remained largely dependent on their trucks and motorcycles.

Changes for Barbarossa

In the preparation for the invasion of the Soviet Union in 1941, a full-scale reorganisation and re-equipment of the panzer arm went ahead. For Operation Barbarossa, as the attack was codenamed, Hitler decided to double the number of panzer divisions available to him, which he managed to do by the simple expedient of halving the tank strength of each division. In Poland, as mentioned above, each division had 328 tanks, but an armoured division that invaded the Soviet Union had one tank regiment of two battalions, a total of 160 tanks. The Type 1941 division also had four battalions of motorised infantry as well as a motorcycle battalion. Clearly, the tank to infantry ratio had changed considerably. Although in 1942 the divisional strength for a panzer division was increased to 200 tanks on paper, the constant casualties, breakdowns and shortages of tanks meant that very few divisions were anywhere near their theoretical strength; many were under half strength. Given this lack of tanks, their infantry component became more and more important.

In June 1942, the *schützen* regiments of the panzer divisions were renamed panzergrenadier regiments. According to Major General Thiess, writing in *Signal*, the German Armed Forces magazine, this was in recognition of their elite status. Even so the infantry component, like the tank complement of the panzer division also decreased. The panzergrenadier battalions were reorganised with four companies rather than the five previously. Thus, a Type 1943 panzer division in theory would hold two panzergrenadier regiments. Each of the regiment's battalions now contained just three rifle companies and the heavy company.

The shortage of tanks was in part compensated for by an increase in firepower for the panzergrenadier regiments, despite their reduction in size. For example, in 1939 a panzer division's three battalions of *schützen* rifle men and battalion of motorcyclists possessed 110 light and 56 heavy machine guns, thirty-six 50mm and twenty-four 80mm mortars, eight light infantry guns and twelve 3.7cm PAK 36 anti-tank guns.

The Germans compensated for the reduction of tanks and also manpower by upping the formation's available weaponry. Its 1944 equivalent, made up of four battalions of panzergrenadiers had 364 light and 49 heavy machine guns, no light 50mm, but twenty-eight 80mm and sixteen

Below: A Sd Kfz 251/10 armed with a 3.7cm gun involved in a hunt for communist partisans in Yugoslavia. Such adaptations were commonplace as a means of giving panzergrenadiers fire support. Alongside is a mortar crew, operating an 8cm sGrW34 mortar.

Above: Panzergrenadiers atop a StuG III assault gun. Assault guns become increasingly common among panzergrenadier formations as the war unfolded, acting as a replacement for the tanks that each division was supposed to possess.

120mm heavy mortars, 12 heavy infantry guns, 40 2cm AA guns and 12 7.5cm infantry guns. The anti-tank guns had been handed over to the division's anti-tank battalion, which had 43 7.5 cm PAK 40 guns. These, however, always worked in close cooperation with the panzergrenadiers.

The *Kampfgruppe* and Type 45 Panzer Division

One of the advantages of the German panzer division was its ability to split up into self-contained components, known as *Kampfgruppe* (battle groups). The division could on occasions prove too unwieldy, so in late 1941 and early 1942, one tank battalion of 40 to 60 tanks, one armoured panzergrenadier battalion equipped with Sd Kfz 251 half tracks, and one artillery battalion were organised into a separate entity within the division. Usually, particularly after 1943, the best elements of the division were concentrated in the *Kampfgruppe* for the purposes of attack and counter-attack. Invariably, the division's best tanks, the halftracks for the panzergrenadiers and Wespe self-propelled artillery pieces were concentrated in this formation. As the war turned against the Germans, these *Kampfgruppe* proved particularly useful, playing the role of so-called fire brigades. They made quick, powerful counter-attacks to stem enemy penetration. Thus, the panzer battle group, although acting in the defensive, was still true to Guderian's original pre-war concept of a

mobile combined arms formation being a balanced mix of artillery, motorised infantry and tanks.

The battle group concept was further refined in the last months of the war, and this reorganisation heightened the importance of the panzergrenadier within Germany's panzer divisions. The Type 45 panzer division of March 1945 had a mixed panzer regiment comprising a panzer battalion and an armoured (halftrack equipped) panzergrenadier battalion. This was complemented by a further two motorised (truck borne) panzergrenadier regiments of two battalions each. The division was completed by a mixed tank-hunter battalion using 75mm PAK anti-tank guns and Jagdpanzers, and an artillery regiment, consisting of one self-propelled battalion using Wespes and Hummels and two motorised battalions equipped with towed artillery pieces.

Although this sounds formidable (and it was) the increased preponderance of panzergrenadiers within the formation should be borne in mind. There were five battalions of infantry as compared with one of tanks; there was even parity in the actual tank regiment which was made up of one tank battalion and one armoured panzergrenadier battalion. It has been argued that this reorganisation was an acceptance by the German High Command that the fighting power of the panzergrenadier matched that of the tank. While not necessarily denying this, it is worth noting that the Type 45 panzer division only had 54 tanks (including its anti-tank battalion's Jagdpanzer tank destroyers) in its theoretical inventory – most divisions had much less. It is worthwhile comparing this to a 1939 Panzer Division with 328 tanks or even a 1941 division with a theoretical strength of 160. Given the constant attrition of available tanks and the inability of German industry to provide enough replacements, it is hardly surprising that the proportion of panzergrenadiers to tanks had risen. This dilution of tank strength was more an acceptance of the fact that by 1945 tanks were increasingly scarce. The changed ratio of tanks to infantry within a panzer division was a matter of enforced necessity rather than a German doctrinal acceptance of equality in firepower between panzergrenadier and tank units.

The Panzergrenadier Division

As noted above, the motorised infantry divisions were just that: infantry formations carried by motorised transport, usually trucks and motorcycles. Although more mobile and thus able to keep up with the panzer divisions spearheading the advance, the motorised divisions were structured along the lines of their regular infantry division counterparts. The manpower and equipment strength of a typical 1939 motorised infantry division was as follows: 16,445 men in total, of which 492 were officers. They were transported by 989 troop trucks, 1627 other lorries, 1323 motorcycles, and 621 motorcycle combinations (these were still an important part of the troops' transport). The reconnaissance battalion had 30 armoured cars. The artillery available included 84 light and 54 medium mortars, 24 light infantry guns, 72 PaK 36 anti-tank guns, 36 light and 12 heavy field howitzers, and 12 20mm anti-aircraft guns.

Although the motorised infantry component was reduced after the Polish campaign, the basic structure of the division did not alter until 1942. In the summer of that year the High Command provided a number of the motorised divisions with a battalion of tanks. This considerably increased the division's combat potential, and proved successful enough for this to become standard practice. Although initially many of these units were equipped with tanks – sometimes Pz Kpfw III and more commonly Pz Kpfw IV – assault guns were far more usual, particularly as the war progressed.

The middle years of the war led to a number of changes of terminology for the motorised divisions. In October 1942 the infantry regiments of the motorised infantry were renamed 'grenadier regiments'. Subsequently, in March 1943, they became known as panzergrenadier regiments. The following year, on 23 June 1943, all the German Army's motorised infantry divisions became panzergrenadier divisions, with the exception of the 14th and 36th Divisions. These were demotorised and reverted to simple infantry formations. The Type 1943 panzergrenadier division of 24 September 1943 consisted, on paper, of headquarters staff, two panzergrenadier regiments, each consisting of three battalions each (this was an increase on the size of a motorised division), an armoured battalion with tanks or more often *Sturmgeschütz* assault guns, an anti-tank battalion (in theory self-propelled), a reconnaissance battalion, an artillery regiment, a flak battalion, a signal battalion and various support formations. The divisional strength was 15,418 men of which 415 were officers. The firepower available to the division consisted of 46 medium and 24 heavy mortars, 14 light and 4 heavy infantry pieces, 21 75mm anti-tank guns,

Below: Panzergrenadiers debus from a lorry after making contact with the enemy on the Eastern Front. These panzergrenadiers would then mount a conventional infantry assault to clear away the opposition, before resuming their advance.

Above: German armour and armoured personnel carriers
assembling for Operation *Zitadelle* (the attack on the Kursk salient)
in the summer of 1943. In the foreground is a Sd Kfz 251 alongside
a Pz Kpfw III.

24 flamethrowers in the hands of the engineers, 42 20mm
and 4 88mm anti-aircraft guns, 18 armoured (usually 20mm
cannon-armed) cars for the reconnaissance battalion, 43
self propelled anti-tank guns and 45 tanks or assault guns.
Given the combat losses endured by many German panzer
divisions by mid 1943, fully-equipped panzergrenadier
divisions often contained as many tanks as their depleted
armoured equivalent.

Type 44 Panzergrenadier Division

In 1944 further reorganisation led to the reduction of 680
men from the theoretical strength of a panzergrenadier
division. In keeping with the German tactical theory of
'few men – many weapons', the firepower in all arms
was increased. There was, of course, one very important
exception: the division's armoured component did not rise as
the shortage of tanks and support guns continued to worsen.
Assault guns replaced any remaining tanks that the division
might hold. The final reorganisation of these divisions
took place in the last desperate months of the war, when in
March 1945 all panzergrenadier divisions ceased to exist as a
separate classification, and they all became panzer divisions
– the 16th Panzer Grenadier Division predated this change

by 11 months when it became the 116th Panzer Division
in May 1944. However, this was little more than a cosmetic
name change because few divisions, be they panzer or
panzergrenadier, had more than a handful of tanks available
to them by this time.

The divisional organisations described above are
essentially theoretical; almost all panzergrenadier formations
contained some variations from the prescribed norm.
However, those variations were largely minor. Two army
panzergrenadier divisions, the elite *Grossdeutschland* and the
Feldherrnhalle were organised differently from the rest and
equipped to a far more lavish scale. The *Grossdeutschland*
Motorised Infantry Division was designated Panzer
Grenadier on 19 May 1943. The division had no less than
four tank and one assault gun battalions. Its inventory on the
eve of the Battle of Kursk in July 1943 was impressive, and
contained a number of Germany's latest models of tanks. At
Kursk *Grossdeutschland* fielded 45 Pz Kpfw IVs, 46 Panthers
(just out of the factory and extremely unreliable), 13 Tigers
and 35 StuG IIIs. *Feldherrnhalle*, which was formed from the
60th Panzer Grenadier Division on 20 June 1943, was also
well equipped. Its original divisional structure had four tank
companies (each with 22 tanks) per battalion rather than the
standard number of three. This soon reverted to three, but
Feldherrnhalle's infantry component was also higher than
that of a standard division. Its panzergrenadier battalions
(known as fusiliers within the division for traditional
reasons) were made up of four companies rather than three.

Admittedly, when the division was later reconstructed after being destroyed at Minsk in July 1944, its battalions consisted of three panzergrenadier companies, which was a standard division's complement.

Of the Waffen SS panzergrenadier divisions, 1st *Leibstandarte*, 2nd *Das Reich*, 3rd *Totenkopf* and 5th *Wiking* were also well equipped with regard to tanks. They each had one regiment of tanks and a battalion of assault guns, which made them stronger than many panzer divisions.

THE EBB AND FLOW OF PANZERGRENADIER DIVISIONS

The Germans had four motorised divisions: the 2nd, 13th, 20th and 29th, at the beginning of the Polish Campaign. The *Grossdeutschland* (motorised) Regiment was formed in the winter of 1939–1940 in time to take part in the invasion of France. The motorised divisions performed well in Poland and also in France, so a further expansion followed after the French campaign in the autumn of 1940. Therefore, 3rd, 10th, 14th, 18th, 25th, 36th and 60th Infantry Divisions were motorised. Also the 16th Motorised Infantry Division was formed from the elements of the 16th Infantry Division which did not go to form the 16th Panzer Division. The 2nd Motorised Division converted to a panzer division in December 1940. In April 1942 the *Grossdeutschland* Regiment was expanded by two regiments, and began the process of expanding to full divisional strength. The major German defeat at Stalingrad in late 1942 and early 1943 resulted in the destruction of the 3rd, 29th and 60th Motorised Infantry Divisions. The 3rd and 28th reformed in France and the 60th was reconstructed in July 1943 as the *Feldherrnhalle* Panzer Grenadier Division.

As mentioned above, on 23 June 1943 all motorised divisions, with the exception of 14th and 36th, were renamed panzergrenadier divisions. In all, 15 army panzergrenadier divisions were formed (see table, page 26).

PANZERGRENADIER TACTICS

Guderian always accepted that tanks could not operate alone effectively. Despite anti-infantry weaponry – usually machine-guns – a tank was always vulnerable to small groups or even lone infantrymen if they were determined enough. This vulnerability was increased if the infantry had access to decent anti-tank guns or devices, but even poorly-equipped foot soldiers could prove to be a real danger if they had the requisite courage. Finnish tank-killing infantry destroyed about 1600 Soviet tanks during the Winter War 1939–40, mostly using Molotov cocktails, or petrol-filled vodka bottles. Tanks proved particularly at risk in broken terrain, such as forests (something the Finns exploited) and urban areas.

When tanks were fighting through defensive lines or moving through landscape that provided the enemy with decent cover, they needed accompanying infantry. Indeed the tanks might require that the infantry go in first to clear the way or make the break through in the enemy line for the tanks to exploit. Thus the panzergrenadier might very often have to fight like a conventional infantryman. Conversely, in a fast-moving advance that characterised German blitzkrieg he might well find himself carried by halftrack, lorry or motorcycle or, in extreme circumstances, hanging from a tank, ready to dismount and engage anything that slowed the tanks. Whenever tanks bypassed points or 'pockets' of stiff enemy resistance, it was the job of the panzergrenadier to clear up these pockets.

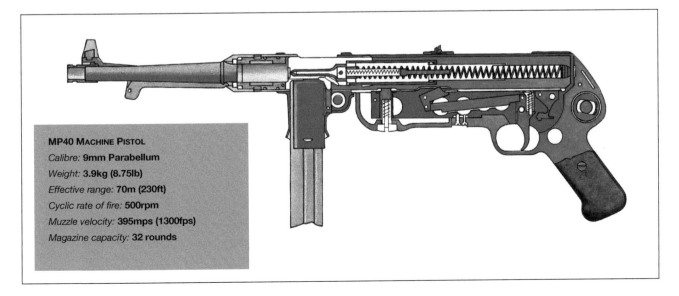

MP40 MACHINE PISTOL
Calibre: **9mm Parabellum**
Weight: **3.9kg (8.75lb)**
Effective range: **70m (230ft)**
Cyclic rate of fire: **500rpm**
Muzzle velocity: **395mps (1300fps)**
Magazine capacity: **32 rounds**

PANZERGRENADIER DIVISIONS

3rd Panzer Grenadier Division fought in Italy and northern Europe following its reconstruction after Stalingrad. It was trapped and destroyed in the Ruhr Pocket in April 1945.

10th Panzer Grenadier Division fought in the east until its remnants surrendered to the Soviets in Czechoslovakia at the end of the War.

15th Panzer Grenadier Division was formed from the remnants of 15th Panzer Division in Sicily in the summer of 1943. It fought with distinction in the Italian campaign but finished the war in northwest Europe.

16th Panzer Grenadier Division served in Yugoslavia and the east until converting to a panzer division in March 1944.

18th Panzer Grenadier Division served in the east, broke out of the encirclement at Minsk and survived long enough to fight in the Battle of Berlin in the last days of the War.

20th Panzer Grenadier Division also fought in the east and Poland, until defending the Seelow Heights outside Berlin, where it was destroyed in May 1945.

25th Panzer Grenadier Division fought in the central sector of the Eastern Front for three years before being transferred to the west for refitting. It fought in the Battle of the Bulge and was then transferred to Berlin during the last Soviet offensive. Most of its survivors, however, managed to escape west and surrender to the British and Americans.

29th Panzer Grenadier Division fought in Poland, France and later the east, where it was destroyed at Stalingrad. The rebuilt Division fought in Italy until destroyed by the British 8th Army in April 1945.

90th Panzer Grenadier Division, which as a light division fought in north Africa, was destroyed in Tunisia in May 1943. The reformed Division fought throughout the Italian campaign and was destroyed near Bologna in April 1945.

Brandenburg **Panzer Grenadier Division** was formed from the Abwehr special forces unit. It fought on the Eastern Front until the end of the War.

Feldherrnhalle **Panzer Grenadier Division** suffered heavily when the massive Soviet summer offensive of 1944 annihilated Army Group Centre. It was finally destroyed during the siege of Budapest.

Grossdeutschland **Panzer Grenadier Division,** was an elite formation that fought exceptionally well throughout the war and was redesignated a panzer division in the winter of 1943–44. It ended the war defending East Prussia.

Kurmark **Panzer Grenadier Division** was an ad-hoc formation, which formed in the last days of the war and never exceeded regimental strength. It was a panzer division in name only.

Führer **Grenadier Division** was organised in early 1945 and fought in the Battle of Vienna as part of Sixth SS Panzer Army.

Führer **Escort Division** was formed originally as an escort battalion for Hitler and was expanded to divisional size in January 1945.

As for the 14 SS panzergrenadier divisions, the 1st, 2nd, 3rd, 5th, 9th, 10th and 12th all became SS panzer divisions in October 1943. The 16th *Reichsführer* SS Panzer Grenadier Division saw service in Italy and Hungary and was destroyed in Vienna in April 1945. The 17th *Götz Von Berlichingen* fought in France and Germany after the Normandy landings. The 18th *Horst Wessel* was formed in Hungary in 1944 and, unlike so many panzergrenadier divisions formed in this period, was properly equipped. It fought in the east, Poland and Slovakia and ended the War in the pocket east of Prague.

23rd SS Panzer Grenadier Division was formed from Dutch SS men in the last weeks of the war and fought in the Battle of Berlin. It never exceeded regimental strength.

34th *Landsturm Nederland* **SS Panzer Grenadier Division** was formed in Germany in 1943 mainly from Dutch personnel. It saw service in Yugoslavia but was transferred to Army Group North in December 1943. It was continuously engaged in the retreat through the Baltic States and ended the war in the Courland pocket. There was also a second parachute *Hermann Göring* Panzer Grenadier Division, which never reached full strength. The term parachute was honorary. It was assigned to the new Parachute Panzer Corps *Hermann Göring* and was smashed in East Prussia in early 1945. Its remnants were transferred south and ended the war in the Prague pocket.

Although the classic image of the panzergrenadier is intimately associated with the Sd Kfz 251 half-tracked armoured personnel carrier, there were never enough of these vehicles to equip panzergrenadier formations to full strength. The concept of a carrier-borne attack into the heart of the enemy's defences accompanying the tanks was the ideal, but the reality was somewhat more mundane. Most panzergrenadiers were transported in soft-skinned vehicles such as trucks and motorcycles. These were extremely vulnerable and thus considerable caution was required when following the tanks. There were no halftracks available in the Polish campaign, and later in the war very few panzergrenadier divisions had many of these vehicles. Even within the panzer divisions, only one battalion in two would be so equipped. Therefore, instead of driving into the midst of the enemy's position, the panzergrenadiers normally debussed at a forming-up point or start line away from the enemy's line of sight. They then attacked in the conventional manner of infantry supporting tanks. The key tactical advantage was that because of their motorisation, they could be brought into battle as soon as they were needed.

It was only at the time of the invasion of the Soviet Union in 1941 that large numbers of Sd Kfz 251s became widely available enough to equip full battalions of panzergrenadiers within panzer divisions. Now, the Germans could experiment with fighting directly from their half-tracks. Although the Sd Kfz 251 provided decent protection against small arms fire, they only had 13mm (0.51in) of armour-plate. Thus, they were extremely vulnerable to even the smallest calibre anti-tank weapons and suffered accordingly. Due to the heavy losses suffered amongst the halftracks when accompanying the tanks into the heart of the battle, the Germans fairly quickly resorted to debussing at least 400m or so in front of the enemy's positions, even when using the Sd Kfz 251. Nonetheless, under certain tactical conditions, the halftrack could provide a useful firing position.

At the lowest level, the basic panzergrenadier unit was the *gruppe* or squad, usually of 12 men mounted in a half-track or often a truck. The squad was led by a squad leader, usually a junior NCO such as a corporal, who was armed with a machine pistol and was responsible for the squad to the platoon commander. On the move, he also commanded the vehicle and fired the vehicle-mounted machine-gun. His rifle-armed assistant was normally a lance corporal, and could lead half the squad if it was divided. The squad contained two light machine-gun teams, each of two men, four rifle-armed infantrymen and the driver and co-driver.

Below: A panzergrenadier section demonstrating the usual method of debussing from an armoured halftrack on the Eastern Front. A machine gun is mounted at the rear of the halftrack for air defence, although it would probably be of little effective use.

The driver was also responsible for the care of the vehicle and expected to remain with the transport. A panzergrenadier platoon was made up of three squads, with the platoon headquarters in a separate vehicle. The headquarters troop consisted of a platoon commander, usually a junior officer but sometimes a sergeant, a driver, a radio operator, two runners, a medic and usually some form of anti-tank gun.

When the squad was transported by a halftrack, the vehicle was mounted from the rear. The deputy squad leader was responsible for closing the door, thus he would sit towards the rear of the vehicle and the squad leader would sit towards the front. These vehicles were open-topped, and on the move it was usual for one man to scan the skies constantly for aircraft, whilst the others kept a watch on both sides of the vehicle. When a platoon was driving together, close order for the convoy was usually 5–10m apart in column or even abreast in open country. In combat, however, the gaps were

> The classic German tactic of a *Kesselschlacht*, or 'Cauldron Battle', where the enemy's defensive positions are outflanked, surrounded, and slowly reduced. This was a particular feature of the invasion of Russia in 1941.

extended to beyond 50m, and ragged lines or chequered formations were used. If the whole battalion was deployed, the preferred formation was often an arrowhead. On the whole, troop-carrying vehicles rarely averaged more than 30km per hour road speed. Even under ideal conditions, a panzer division was not expected to advance more than 200km (124 miles) in a day.

The Sd Kfz 251 drivers were prepared to simply ignore or drive through small arms fire, but the presence of enemy artillery or anti-tank guns usually forced the halftracks to seek cover. The squad's machine-gunners might well engage targets on the move, as could the rest of the squad if necessary from the sides of the vehicle. Often when advancing, the Sd Kfz 251s could utilise a motorised version of fire and movement, advancing, stopping and firing to cover the other halftracks. A halted halftrack provided a decent fire platform but was extremely vulnerable. As a result, it was not recommended to stop for more than 15–25 seconds in hostile terrain. The normal dismounting procedure was through the rear of the vehicle. However, in emergencies, the squad might well jump over the sides as well as out of the back. This was often performed on the move at slow speeds. Once dismounted, the panzergrenadiers fought as normal

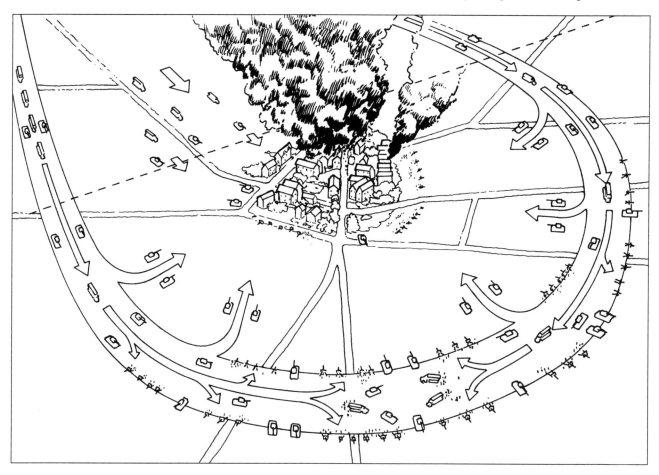

Above: A fully loaded halftrack with abundant reserves of ammunition for the MG34 machine gun. The Germans relied heavily on machine gun fire support in battle, although panzergrenadiers rarely fought from inside their vehicles.

infantry. Improvements in Soviet anti-tank defences as the war advanced meant that the panzergrenadiers often had to precede the tanks, or a mixed force of tanks and soldiers might move forward to clear the enemy defences.

One of the most important German formations developed during the Soviet campaign was the *pulk*, a contraction of *panzer und lastkraftwagen*, meaning tanks and trucks. This was a hollow wedge of tanks inside which moved the motorised infantry. The point of the wedge was formed by the best tanks and the sides by other tanks and self-propelled guns. When the wedge pierced the enemy defences, it widened the gap as it passed through. The motorised infantry were then able to spread out and attack any remaining areas of resistance from the flank and rear. If the enemy's weakest point had not been identified, the *pulk* could advance as a blunt quadrangle. Once a weak spot was found, the formation could incline left or right, its corner becoming the point of advance.

Although the panzergrenadiers' key role was cooperation with tanks, they could also operate on their own. Their very flexibility was a vital component of their value. They could fight traditional infantry offensive and defensive actions, assault vital strongpoints, seize bridges and clear urban or wooded areas in which tanks were vulnerable. Essentially, the panzergrenadier was part of an all-arms team. His role had grown out of the German acceptance that the tank could not win battles alone. To quote Wilhelm Necker in 1943: 'The Germans at an early stage of the war and even before the war understood the special weakness of the tank: its dependency on terrain and the fact it cannot occupy, but can only strike hard and break through the lines. For this reason, the actual tank force was cut down to the very minimum and the division reinforced with various other units, the most important of which is the Panzer Grenadier regiment.' How these regiments performed is recounted in the next two chapters.

CHAPTER 3

Panzergrenadiers in Action in the West, 1939–45

Although the invasion of Poland saw the first use of motorised infantry, the 1940 French campaign showed the German blitzkrieg tactics to full effect. Conversely, by 1944, the panzergrenadiers proved themselves highly skilled at delaying the Allied advance through France and the Low Countries.

PANZERGRENADIERS were used throughout World War II, from the invasion of Poland in September 1939, to the battle for Berlin in April 1945. As a fighting elite accompanying the panzers into action, or as infantry fighting stubborn rearguard actions, they were typically engaged in the thickest fighting of the war. They fought in both offensive and defensive mode; as the war went against Germany from 1942–43 it was increasingly in the latter role that they were deployed. Throughout the war, some of the best units of the German armed forces fought as panzergrenadiers. These included the *Grossdeutschland* Division, 1st SS *Leibstandarte Adolf Hitler* Division, 2nd SS *Das Reich* Division, 12th SS *Hitler Jugend* Division, the *Brandenburg* Division and the Luftwaffe's elite *Hermann Göring* Division. Although many of these panzergrenadier divisions were later reorganised as panzer divisions, even with such reorganisation, all panzer divisions, including elite formations such as the Wehrmacht's *Panzer Lehr* Division, always had attached panzergrenadier regiments that would go into battle with the armour.

To make sense of the widely spread theatres of war in which panzergrenadiers fought, the two chapters on the panzergrenadiers' war record will focus firstly on the war in the West, before examining events on the Eastern Front in the next chapter. With this in mind, this chapter will deal briefly with the invasion of Poland before examining two case studies in which panzergrenadiers were heavily involved: firstly, the elite *Grossdeutschland* Regiment's offensive action in Operation Niwi and across the river Meuse at the battle of Sedan in May 1940 during the Fall of France; secondly, the defensive action of the 12th SS *Hitler Jugend* (Hitler Youth) Panzer Division in Normandy in 1944. Chapter Four will then cover the panzergrenadiers' war on the Eastern Front by examining three pertinent case studies: firstly, the German advance on Moscow following Operation Barbarossa when it looked as though Germany would capture Moscow and conquer the USSR; secondly, panzergrenadiers in action during the battle of Kursk in 1943, the biggest tank battle of the war, with over 6000 tanks and self-propelled guns involved, where the Soviets halted the German advance; finally, panzergrenadiers in a defensive role on the borders of Germany in 1944 as the Red Army steamrollered west into Poland and Germany. These case studies provide accounts of panzergrenadiers in a variety of different theatres of war, and show how the panzergrenadier performed in attack as well as defence. As will be seen, whether fighting in the woods of the Ardennes, the bocage of Normandy, or the steppes of the Soviet Union, German panzergrenadiers invariably proved the maxim of the German army commander of the 1920s, Hans von Seekt: '*Mehr seins als Schein*' ('Be more than you appear to be').

Left: SS panzergrenadiers from *Kampfgruppe* Hansen smoking captured American Camel cigarettes, somewhere in the Ardennes during the Battle of the Bulge, 1944. Behind them is a knocked-out American M8 armoured car.

MOTORISED INFANTRY VS PANZERGRENADIER

As has been seen in the chapters on organisation and training, the term 'panzergrenadier' is ambiguous. When Germany entered the war in September 1939, the Wehrmacht and Waffen SS had motorised infantry divisions. These units had evolved in stages from motorised infantry regiments of the 1930s. As the SS were expected to be in the van of any assault, and as the SS creamed off the best of Germany's new military equipment, they were usually motorised. Having said this, at the beginning of the war the SS motorised 'divisions' were often sub-divisional regimental formations in the process of being built into divisional-sized units. These motorised units became panzergrenadier divisions from 1942–43 as the war on the Eastern Front led to changes in the German armed forces. Some of these panzergrenadier divisions, particularly the SS divisions and the *Grossdeutschland*, ended up with such a large armoured core that they were renamed 'panzer' divisions in 1943 and 1944. To complicate matters, some of the motorised divisions went through an intermediate phase of being a panzergrenadier division before becoming a full panzer division; meanwhile, some panzergrenadier divisions that became panzer divisions kept

the name 'panzergrenadier'. In addition, it should be borne in mind that panzer divisions throughout the war had an organic component of motorised infantry carried in lorries and armoured personnel carriers (APCs). As will be seen, it was with panzer divisions as much as panzergrenadier divisions that panzergrenadiers fought during World War II. Finally, it is worth remembering that panzergrenadier divisions from 1942 were further divided into motorised and mechanised formations, with a motorised division having fewer APCs and more lorries, while a mechanised division had more tanks and APCs.

Therefore, in the two chapters on panzergrenadiers in action, the reader should be aware of some imprecision in the term 'panzergrenadier'. Before the invasion of the USSR and the wide-spread development of panzergrenadier divisions, the terms 'motorised' and 'panzergrenadier' will be used interchangeably. What can be asserted with certainty is that the motorised infantry used in the campaigns in Poland, France and the Balkans from 1939 to 1941 were the direct forerunners of the panzergrenadier divisions of the later stages of World War II.

THE INVASION OF POLAND, 1939

When Germany invaded Poland in September 1939, the first dramatic example of the power of blitzkrieg or 'lightning war', three motorised corps spearheaded the attack. Included were four motorised divisions.

Below: Panzergrenadiers in a halftrack armed with anti-aircraft gun negotiate a muddy track during the invasion of Poland. Anti-aircraft protection for panzergrenadiers was continually strengthened as the war progressed.

Left: An officer of the *Grossdeutschland* Division, the cream of the Wehrmacht, scans the horizon. Members of the *Grossdeutschland* were called on to perform a variety of combat tasks throughout the war, and deserved their reputation as skilled opponents.

impeded the advance. Most points of resistance were left for the infantry marching up from the rear to tackle. The motorised infantry were there to facilitate the speed of the armoured advance.

CASE STUDY ONE: THE FALL OF FRANCE, 1940

The invasion of France on May 1940 presented the panzergrenadier with a more formidable proposition: the French and British forces facing the Germans actually outnumbered the Germans in terms of numbers of tanks and aeroplanes. What would give the Germans success in one of the most dramatic campaigns of World War II was their superior tactics and motivation. The Germans directed their main weight of attack (the *schwerpunkt*) through the wooded Ardennes area of Belgium that the Allied forces believed to be impassable for a large armoured force. The aim was to bypass and trap the main body of French and British forces advancing to the north into central Belgium. The Germans' objective was to cross the river Meuse at Sedan, advance to the English Channel and encircle the British and French forces in Belgium. The plan worked and led to the withdrawal of the British Expeditionary Force from Dunkirk and the collapse of France in June 1940. To make the plan succeed, the Germans had to get their men and tanks rapidly across the formidable river obstacle of the Meuse. On the hilly west bank, entrenched French units waited to block any attempt at a river crossing.

Panzer Grenadier Regiment *Grossdeutschland*

To cross the Meuse, the Germans deployed the Wehrmacht's elite panzergrenadier unit: the *Grossdeutschland* Regiment (that would become the *Grossdeutschland* Panzer Grenadier Division and then the *Grossdeutschland* Panzer Corps).The *Grossdeutschland* was one of the Wehrmacht's crack units, comparable in fighting ability and equipment provision to any SS unit. From 1940 to 1945 their story was one of almost continuous front-line service. Like the British Brigade of Guards, the men of the *Grossdeutschland* had to be over a certain height and the *Grossdeutschland* always fought as a separate unit. On the sleeve of every grenadier of the *Grossdeutschland* was emblazoned the name '*Grossdeutschland*'. The unit could trace its origins back to

Also present were SS motorised regiments *Adolf Hitler, Deutschland* and *Germania*. With the addition of four 'light' divisions that became panzer divisions after the Poland campaign, the Germans deployed the equivalent of some six motorised divisions against the Polish forces. In addition, all the panzer divisions, as has been noted, had a motorised infantry brigade attached to support the armoured assault. These motorised troops were crucial to the whole concept of blitzkrieg. Compared with the later battles on the Eastern Front, the numbers of panzergrenadiers deployed were small but, as the military historian J.F.C. Fuller noted in his history of the Second World War, their influence on operations was 'decisive'.

At this stage, the motorised infantry was largely lorry borne. Later, armoured vehicles would take the panzergrenadiers into battle with more safety and would allow them to get closer to the action. Nevertheless, when the Germans invaded Poland, the motorised infantry formed a key part of the all-arms effort that was blitzkrieg. While Luftwaffe Ju-87 'Stukas' pounded the Polish front-line positions and rear areas, the armoured tip to the blitzkrieg pushed into and through the Polish lines. In the initial phases of the battle for Poland, the Germans avoided areas of tough resistance. Advancing in a wedge formation, German tanks were supported by their motorised infantry that helped clear the way and stormed vital positions that

Above: A Fieseler-Storch Fi 156 light plane. This aeroplane was typically used for army cooperation and reconnaisance, but in Operation Niwi in 1940 it took an active role, ferrying men from *Grossdeutschland* into action.

the Berlin 'Guard Regiment' of the 1870s, and during the 1920s it had been employed to keep order in the German capital. In peacetime, the task of the regiment was to march, three times a week and with the band playing *Deutschland über Alles*, to change the guard at the Brandenburger Tor in Berlin. The regiment provided the guard of honour when foreign dignitaries visited Germany. A detachment from the *Grossdeutschland*, the *Führer Begleit*, also provided a personal bodyguard for Adolf Hitler. The *Grossdeutschland* was a natural choice for the task of being motorised infantry, and France 1940 would be the unit's baptism of fire.

The commander of the push through the Ardennes, Heinz Guderian, had earmarked the *Grossdeutschland* for two tasks in the battle for France: firstly, Operation Niwi, a special forces mission behind enemy lines; secondly, and more crucially, the role of smashing through the French lines on the Meuse to open the way for the German panzers to sweep across to the English Channel.

Operation Niwi
Operation Niwi proved that panzergrenadiers were well suited for a variety of tasks, not just armoured support. One battalion of the *Grossdeutschland*, the 3rd, was removed from the armoured thrust through the Ardennes and given the task of capturing the Belgian towns of *Nives* and *Witry* (hence the codename for the operation) to aid the drive of the 1st and 2nd Panzer Divisions through the Belgian lines. To reach their objectives, the men of the 3rd Battalion, commanded by Lt Col Eugen Garski, would be transported behind the lines by a fleet of light Fieseler Storch aeroplanes. Once in place the men would be resupplied by Ju-52 transport aircraft.

The men on Operation Niwi trained hard for the operation and received a personal visit from Hitler, who assured them of his faith in their abilities. As is so often the way, nothing on Operation Niwi went according to plan. The Fieseler Storch aircraft got lost and dispersed, and only a small number of men reached their objective. However, the dislocation and surprise of the Belgians allowed the Germans to gather their forces and block Belgian troop movements. Operation Niwi was not a great success but it proved that panzergrenadiers in units such as the *Grossdeutschland* could be used as special forces. It also shows that it is wrong to assume that panzergrenadiers only fought in close support of armour. Panzergrenadiers could be employed in a variety of tasks not classically associated with the role of motorised infantry. For instance, the *Brandenburg* Panzer Grenadier Division started life as a special forces unit designed for clandestine operations, and as such was involved in some of the most daring special commando-style operations of the war.

The battle to cross the Meuse
Grossdeutschland's most famous task in May 1940 was spearheading the crossing of the river Meuse by 1st Panzer Division. With the return of the 3rd Battalion from Operation Niwi, the *Grossdeutschland* Regiment prepared for the difficult task of an opposed river crossing. Interestingly, the river crossing meant that it was the infantry, supported by German tanks and the Luftwaffe, that would spearhead the assault. Normally, the tanks would punch through the enemy lines and carry through the motorised infantry; at the Meuse in 1940 it was the other way round. Again, this shows how panzergrenadier were expected to function in a variety of different combat roles.

For the assault, the *Grossdeutschland* Regiment arrived by lorry and took up assault positions along the eastern bank of the Meuse. The assault showed the versatility of motorised infantry: the men of the *Grossdeutschland* would have to paddle in rubber dinghies across a wide river in the face of French bunkers, guns and entrenched infantry, to secure a bridgehead for the panzers. To do this the panzergrenadiers would have to advance through the French fortified defences on the western bank of the Meuse, knocking out the bunkers and pillboxes as they went.

At midday on 13 May the shock elements of *Grossdeutschland* were issued with iron rations and flasks of coffee. The stillness before the assault struck the assaulting troops. Second Lieutenant Courbiere, commanding No 6 Company, recalled how on the east bank: 'Not a shot falls, the inhabitants have fled, dogs and cats roam through the streets whose destroyed houses bear witness to the fearful force of the war.' Courbiere wondered whether the silence meant that the French on the west bank had gone. He was quickly disabused of this idea. As they saw the combat engineers and assault troops of the *Grossdeutschland* approach the river bank, the French opened up with small arms and artillery fire from their bunkers and gun positions on the west bank. As Courbiere remembered, the Germans brought up assault guns and tanks to provide close fire support for the men crossing the river: 'but their shells can do nothing against the concrete and iron. Valuable time is lost, until finally a heavy 88mm. flak silences the enemy. Once again the assault boats are brought up, but this attempt also brings down enemy fire. The young lieutenant of the 7th Company, Lieutenant Graf Medem and two engineers are killed. The wounded are brought back – once again a heavy flak is brought into action. Under its protection the first sections of the leading (No.7) company cross the Meuse. The crossing has succeeded! Swiftly, as we had already practised in the winter, 6th Company follows.' This quotation shows the importance of

all-arms action that was the blitzkrieg. The panzergrenadiers were brought up in lorries and were supported in their crossing by combat engineers, heavy anti-aircraft guns (the ubiquitous '88') and as much aerial support as the Luftwaffe could bring to bear on the Meuse. The element of rigorous training is also evident: the men had been practising for just such a river crossing for many months. All these factors combined to make the German crossing of the Meuse successful.

All along the river Meuse by Sedan, German motorised infantry paddled the width of the river in rubber boats, frantically trying to reach the opposite bank before French defenders blew them out of the water. At the same time German panzers, positioned right on the river's edge, did what they could with their main armament and machine guns to suppress the French defenders. In many sectors, German tanks drove slowly up and down the river's edge firing as they went. One account from Captain König of Erwin Rommel's 7th Panzer Division recalled how the tanks fired at ranges of 100 yards and directly engaged the enemy bunkers: 'The fire of the Panzer guns, the 75mm shells as well as the scattered 20mm quick-firing cannon, soon show an effect... the companies shoot almost as if they were in training, and no recognised target, no suspicious movement of the enemy

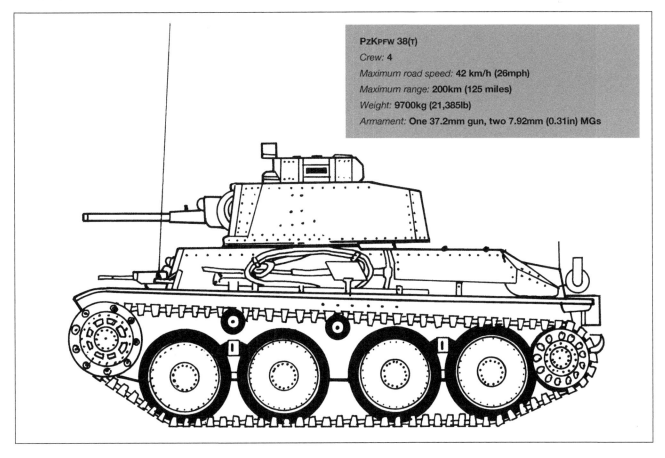

PzKpfw 38(t)
Crew: **4**
Maximum road speed: **42 km/h (26mph)**
Maximum range: **200km (125 miles)**
Weight: **9700kg (21,385lb)**
Armament: **One 37.2mm gun, two 7.92mm (0.31in) MGs**

goes unnoticed. The enemy fire begins to slacken noticeably, but nevertheless the crossing of the first storm boats, the engineers, remains a hard task, a task from which many don't come back. In impotent rage, the tank crews watch boats torn to pieces by direct hits.'

While the tanks remained static, the men of the *Grossdeutschland* (and 1st Motorised Rifle Regiment) attempted to consolidate the bridgehead. The panzergrenadiers operated within the German military tradition of *auftragstaktik* (mission-oriented tactics), which

Above: SS panzergrenadiers crossing a river. River crossings were extremely hazardous and costly operations, and required large amounts of courage, as those crossing the river were extremely exposed to any defensive enemy fire.

allowed junior officers and NCOs to react to the situation on the ground, and ignore orders if they thought their actions would help achieve the unit's mission.

The Ju-87 Stuka dive-bomber was invaluable in providing mobile fire support for the attacking infantry at the Meuse.

Stukas dropped their bombs a 'hair's breadth' from the attacking Germans as they stormed the French defences on the slopes of the hill of La Marfée. The French defenders, many of whom were raw conscripts, were left bewildered by the ferocity of the German bombardment. The ensuing battle for the west bank shows that panzergrenadiers often fought fixed piece assaults on prepared defences. This was classic infantry action. Courbiere again: 'After a short fight the bunker is reached by a sergeant and two men. The enemy are smoked out by hand grenades; they are completely vanquished; they come out. Their faces reveal the psychological strain of this fighting. Close to each other they stand with their backs to their bunker and raise their hands.' In the savage fighting, some of the French defenders in the bunkers were shot after they had surrendered. The panzergrenadiers cleared out bunker after bunker so there would be a foothold on the west bank sufficiently large for

combat engineers to build ferries and a bridge onto which the panzers could pass. All along the Meuse, the experience of the men of the *Grossdeutschland* was repeated as other Wehrmacht motorised infantry units paddled across the river in the face of fierce French fire. Casualties in such an assault were high and for men wounded on the west bank the delay in ferrying them back to regimental aid posts on the east bank often proved fatal. Another problem was the lack of water, and the Germans relied on captured bottles of water to keep them going.

Combat Engineers at the Crossing of the Meuse

The *Grossdeutschland* was just one motorised infantry regiment crossing the Meuse. The experience of the other motorised infantry crossing the river was very similar to that of the *Grossdeutschland*. But it was an all-arms

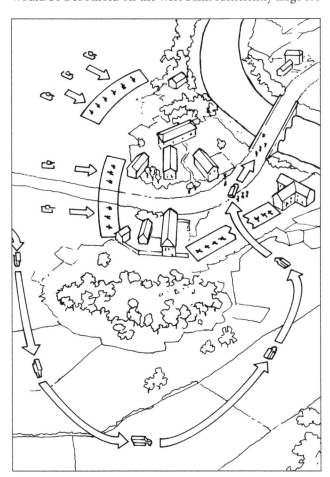

A common blitzkrieg tactic: whilst the German tanks fixed the bridge's defenders with their support fire, the panzergrenadiers would outflank the position, and race through the defences to capture the bridge intact.

Should the bridge be blown, tanks would again provide supporting fire with the panzergrenadiers, while the pioneers attempted to cross the river in rubber boats. Once across, they would seize a bridgehead, and build an assault bridge.

endeavour and it is worth stressing that the first men across the Meuse were invariably combat engineers attached to the motorised infantry. Corporal Frömmel, with the panzers on the east bank, gives a vivid description of the role of the combat engineers who worked in conjunction with the panzergrenadiers: 'The engineers leap off and attempt under this hail of fire to get their boat to the Meuse. There are only a few metres separating them from the bank, and yet each step means hell. The tank shoots with all its guns, it attempts to give fire cover to the determinedly working engineers. The boat is already in the water, its paddles cutting deep into it. Like a shower, a machine-gun bursts from the bunker and falls on this single boat. All around it the water springs up high, and several brave engineers are killed. It is impossible! Back! They come back to the bank and attempt to find cover in the deep grass. The same fate occurs several minutes later to men whose inflatable dinghy has been brought down by three further tanks to this death-dealing river.' Ultimately, it was the determination of engineers and panzergrenadiers to cross in the face of this overwhelming firepower that maintained the momentum of the German offensive.

Below: Infantry advancing with a Czech-built Pz Kpfw 38(t) pressed into German service after the invasion of Czechoslovakia in 1939. These tanks were used in large numbers by the 7th and 8th Panzer Divisions in both France and Russia.

Without the motorised infantry, almost all carried by lorry at this stage of the war, the blitzkrieg would have foundered. Panzergrenadiers were vital instruments in the fall of France. If the Germans had waited for conventional foot-borne infantry to arrive, the French would have had valuable time to prepare for the assault. As it was, the panzergrenadiers arrived with the tanks and could attack almost immediately. Once across the Meuse, the panzer again came into its own and raced across France to reach the Channel on 20 May 1940. The crossing of the Meuse allowed the Germans to break the French defences and morale. This was achieved not by armour, but by determined motorised infantry assault, supported it must be said by combat engineers, tank fire, artillery support from '88s' and, especially, Luftwaffe support from Stuka dive bombers, protected by Bf109 and Bf110 fighter planes.

CASE STUDY TWO: NORMANDY, 1944

The battle for Normandy in 1944 provides an interesting contrast to the fall of France. In May 1940 the Germans were riding on a wave of military success; by 1944, the end of Hitler's Third Reich was in sight. In between, the panzergrenadiers had fought a long and bitter war on the Eastern Front. Meanwhile, in the West in 1944, panzergrenadiers were involved once again, this time in

a defensive role, in containing the Allied beachhead in Normandy established after the D-Day landings of 6 June. In the sunken roads and hedgerows of Normandy, German panzergrenadiers attempted to block an Allied breakout. One of the most famous, indeed infamous, units involved in the battle for Normandy was the 12th SS *Hitler Jugend* Panzer Division.

The 12th SS *Hitler Jugend* Division

The *Hitler Jugend* Division was originally formed as a panzergrenadier division, changing designation to a full panzer division in time to fight in Normandy. It was a peculiar formation. The division comprised former members of the Hitler Youth, trained and led by a cadre of NCOs and officers transferred from the 1st SS *Leibstandarte* Division. This gave the unit both ideological zeal and excellent training, and made them formidable and ruthless opponents in combat. The *Hitler Jugend* Division was also supplied, like most SS units, with the latest equipment, such as heavy tanks and APCs for the panzergrenadiers.

The training provided by the NCOs and officers of the *Leibstandarte* for the *Hitler Jugend* Division was realistic and prepared the division for battle. The training was unconventional, but gave the men an edge over their opponents in Normandy. The instructors from the *Liebstandarte*, veterans of the Eastern Front, eschewed drill and formal parades in favour of realistic battle training: every lesson and exercise had a purpose and had to be conducted as if the squad were actually in battle. This was standard training for all SS soldiers, but it was taken to an extreme with the *Hitler Jugend*. Thus, when the young panzergrenadiers went into battle in 1944 they were already accustomed to the noises and strains of combat. They had already been fired upon with live rounds on the training ground; indeed, a proportion of training deaths was considered 'normal' and necessary to make the soldiers battle effective. The military historian Max Hastings recalled how one of the signals officers in the *Hitler Jugend* felt that 'They had received a proper training in the Hitler Youth. They had a sense of order and discipline. They knew how to sing!' They had also trained for a rapid move to the Normandy beachhead time and time again. The youth of the men of the division was striking: they were given a chocolate ration in lieu of the more usual cigarette ration. It was these ideologically-driven, determined and well-trained panzergrenadiers who went with their panzers to the

Above: With the standard issue Kar 98K rifle, a panzergrenadier in a camouflage smock takes aim. Contrary to common perception, many panzergrenadiers were armed with rifles rather than machine pistols.

Normandy countryside around the town of Caen to face the British and Canadians.

The 12th SS *Hitler Jugend* Division into battle

As the *Hitler Jugend* moved into action, Allied fighter-bombers harried the long columns of vehicles all the way to the front. The training of the division was such that it maintained a good distance between vehicles and this reduced losses from the air attacks. However, Allied air superiority disrupted all German movement and provided Allied forces with close air support throughout the battle for Normandy. This marked a real change from the Meuse crossing, when the Luftwaffe dominated the skies over Sedan. In Normandy, the bombardment from the heavy guns of Allied ships offshore also came as a nasty and novel surprise for all, including the NCOs and officers from the Eastern Front. The determination of the *Hitler Jugend* was evident. Rudolf Schaaf of the 1716th Artillery recalled how 'the SS showed that they believed that thus far, everybody had been fighting like milkmaids.' Schaaf watched the bleak young men of the *Hitler Jugend* move towards the front line, to see them return in tears the same evening. But these tears were not from the strain of battle, but because they had failed to reach their objective and drive the Allies into the sea.

On 7 June, the *Hitler Jugend* panzergrenadiers were given their orders: to drive the enemy back into the sea with an attack that was to go in at midday. Through the night lorries brought the panzergrenadiers to the town of Caen. Once at Caen, the men debussed and made a night march through the town to take up their assault positions. Artillery officers moved ahead to find vantage points to direct the artillery of the division; the 150 tanks of the division did their best to deploy with the panzergrenadiers. The air attacks and general confusion surrounding the deployment of the *Hitler Jugend* panzers and panzergrenadiers meant that the concentration for the attack was far from ideal: divisional cohesion broke down and men moved to the front as best as they could. The tanks, meanwhile, became clogged in the rear as they tried to push forward to the start line for the attack. Once in attack position, the *Hitler Jugend* dug slit trenches and fire pits; everything was camouflaged to avoid the attention of Allied fighter-bombers, before the men could finally grab a few hours of much-needed sleep.

But everything was not going according to plan. The 26th Regiment of the *Hitler Jugend*, with all its tanks, had run out of fuel 22 miles east of the river Orne. In the

Below: France 1944: panzergrenadiers being ferried into battle along the narrow Normandy hedgerows. The camouflage was an attempt to avoid detection by roving Allied fighter-bombers. Allied air superiority over the beachhead was total.

end, when it came to attack on the 7 June, only the three battalions of the 25th Panzer Grenadier Regiment were ready. It was this small force, supported by two panzer detachments that would have to drive the Allies into the sea.

Panzergrenadier versus Canadian infantry

Before this attack could happen, the men of the *Hitler Jugend* heard the noise of tanks approaching: these were light Stuart tanks of the 9th Canadian Brigade. It was now that the training of the unit came to the fore. The risk with untrained troops was that they would open fire prematurely and warn opponents of their presence. The *Hitler Jugend* held their fire and allowed the Canadian tanks to pass. Once this had happened, Panzer IVs appeared from the reverse slope and engaged the Canadian armour. German anti-tank guns then entered the fray. Meanwhile, the panzergrenadiers were given the job of dealing with the Canadian infantry following up the armoured thrust.

The ferocity of the SS panzergrenadier assault pushed the Canadians back to their start line at the towns of St. Contest and Buron. The fighting see-sawed backwards and forwards: the *Hitler Jugend* captured Buron, only to lose it to a charge by Nova Scotia infantry late in the afternoon.

The panzergrenadiers had proved their worth and versatility (as at the crossing of the Meuse). They had moved from a watching position to an aggressive defence and finally to a counter-attack that had pushed the Canadians back to their start line. What stopped the panzergrenadiers was the immense weight of fire support that the Canadians could call upon. Air, sea and land fire support pounded the panzergrenadiers and halted their counter-attacks. All-in-all, the hastily deployed and incomplete *Hitler Jugend* panzergrenadiers and panzers had performed well in halting the Canadian advance, even if they had failed to destroy the Allied beachhead.

Losses had, however, been heavy and with well trained troops losses were hard to replace. This was especially so with regard to the officers of the division, many of whom had been lost leading from the front. The *Hitler Jugend* now settled down into a defensive position to deny the Allies the breakout they desired.

In their battle with the Canadians, the ideologically-driven SS panzergrenadiers took war to its extremes and frequently shot POWs. In return, the Canadians were understandably loath to take SS prisoners. In these battles the Canadians gave as good as they got and showed themselves to be the match of the *Hitler Jugend* Division. Subsequent battles between the two sides saw vicious small unit actions in the bocage and hamlets of Normandy. Every panzergrenadier success was met with a hastily organised Canadian counter-attack. Villages were won and lost; Canadian riflemen armed with the PIAT anti-tank weapon took on *Hitler Jugend* panzers in the close confines of the bocage.

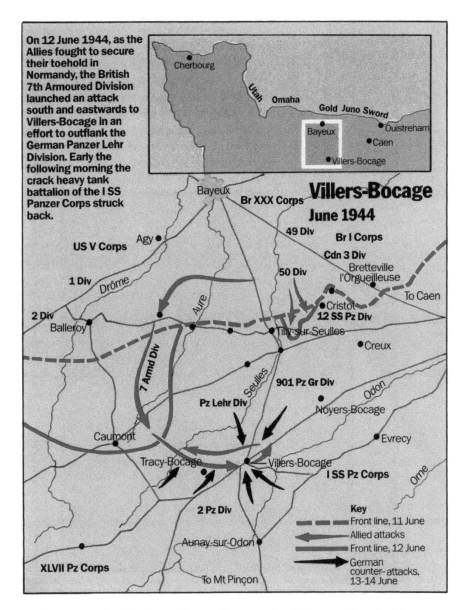

On 12 June 1944, as the Allies fought to secure their toehold in Normandy, the British 7th Armoured Division launched an attack south and eastwards to Villers-Bocage in an effort to outflank the German Panzer Lehr Division. Early the following morning the crack heavy tank battalion of the I SS Panzer Corps struck back.

Normandy: a war of attrition

This was attritional war, reminiscent of World War I, and showed how the panzergrenadier could be expected to fight both in defence and attack. After 7 June the Germans could only hope to contain the Allied beachhead, not destroy it, and the *Hitler Jugend* moved into a defensive deployment. The panzergrenadiers set about laying mines and booby traps, and they built extensive and formidable field fortifications. The ensuing war of attrition, conducted with little or no air support, drained the *Hitler Jugend* Division of its strength. Losses were particularly high amongst junior officers. The battle bled the division and shows the importance of measuring divisional performance with the overall course of the war. No matter how well the panzergrenadiers of the *Hitler Jugend* or other German units fought, with the Third Reich in decline such efforts could only postpone Germany's eventual defeat.

By 1944, Germany was so weak that the *Hitler Jugend* received few replacements for lost men and equipment. Roving Allied air patrols interdicted the replacements that were sent, and in practice frequently destroyed the exiguous replacements before they even reached the Normandy front. In the end, the battle for Normandy destroyed the *Hitler Jugend* Division as a unit.

Panzergrenadiers versus the British

Nonetheless, the remnants of the *Hitler Jugend* division held on in Normandy. The Canadians were replaced by British units which launched a series of offensives to take Caen. These offensives were preceded by intense bombardments to 'soften up' the German positions. It was these attacks that tested the nerve of the panzergrenadier in defence. As has been seen for the Canadian attack on 7 June, the panzergrenadier had to withstand intense artillery and aerial barrages and still be

ready to fight. On 17 June, when attacked by British units, the panzergrenadiers were subjected to a massive bombardment. However, small numbers of the men survived in fox holes and shell craters and engaged the enemy tanks and infantry

Below: In his foxhole, an SS panzergrenadier of the *Hitler Jugend* Division awaits an Allied assault. The Allies had overwhelming firepower in Normandy, yet the panzergrenadiers fought on against all the odds.

with small arms and *Panzerfaust* hand-held anti-tank rockets. The trick of the panzergrenadiers, which required nerves of steel, was to let the tanks pass them by before emerging to attack the tanks from the rear. Small groups would also, as with the Japanese in the Pacific, remain hidden to emerge later to snipe and harry troops in rear areas. The British attack on 17 June was partially successful, but achieved at a heavy cost: 55 killed and 110 wounded. Once established in their new positions, the British were then subjected to continual counter-attacks. The British were eventually forced back to their start lines following a concerted counter-attack by *Hitler Jugend* panzergrenadiers supported by some Panther tanks and self-propelled guns.

Panzergrenadier losses

Losses in these intense engagements were such that command frequently fell on an NCO of any rank. Eventually, weight of numbers began to tell, as Allied reinforcements poured into the beachhead, while German reinforcements arrived in fits and starts. The British made repeated attacks against the *Hitler Jugend* lines, each one repulsed at heavy cost. The fighting in the houses and hamlets of the bocage proved to be as deadly as the Eastern Front. The panzergrenadiers were by this stage exhausted, short of supplies and soaked from early rains. Yet they still employed the tactics of the Eastern Front to deadly effect. In defence, the panzergrenadiers would hold their fire until the last possible moment to make sure they obtained a 'kill'. Then, before British artillery could range in, the panzergrenadiers would move to a new position. This had the effect of making the British think that they were facing an enemy stronger than was really the case. It was also a tactic that required patience and one that exhausted the panzergrenadiers, who had to move around the battlefield and fight continuously in a series of running engagements.

The battle for Normandy became a battle of numbers, a *guerre d'usure*, and no matter how well the panzergrenadiers performed, the superiority in Allied men and equipment would carry the day. The interdiction of German supply lines meant that only limited supplies were reaching the front-line units. Counter-attacks became impossible, not just because the exhausted and battered panzergrenadiers needed sleep, but because there were insufficient shells for an attack.

The end of the *Hitler Jugend* Division: the Falaise Gap

When the German line eventually broke, after months of heavy fighting, the *Hitler Jugend* Division was a shadow of the unit that had gone into battle on 7 June 1944. As it retreated through the Falaise Gap, the Allies pounded the retreating

Above: Infantry advance through the Normandy bocage. Although the terrain did not favour armoured operations, it was perfect for the dogged defensive tactics the Germans were forced to employ in the face of the overwhelming Allied air superiority.

Germans with everything they had. Lieutenant Walter Kruger, a signals officer in the *Hitler Jugend*, remembered how on the Falaise road during the retreat whole columns were on fire as Allied fighter-bombers strafed the Germans. 'Everybody was running' recalled Kruger. Few *Hitler Jugend* panzergrenadiers survived the battle. Kurt Meyer, who took charge of the *Hitler Jugend* when its commander, Fritz Witt, was killed, escaped. However, while a fanatical Nazi and determined soldier, Meyer was badly shaken by the defeat. Considering the shambles behind him, the usually steadfast Meyer admitted: 'My knees trembled, the sweat pouring down my face, my clothes soaked in perspiration.' Meyer and the *Hitler Jugend* were the ultimate expression of fanatical Nazism and as panzergrenadiers they proved to be, perhaps, the toughest opposition of the war. Max Hastings' conclusion that 'No formation caused the Allies such deep trouble in Normandy until the end as the 12th SS Panzer', says much about these panzergrenadiers.

CHAPTER 4

Panzergrenadiers in Action on the Eastern Front, 1941–45

The wide open spaces of Russia proved a perfect demonstration ground for the panzergrenadiers' new style of combat. Equipped with lorries or the latest APCs, they moved from flashpoint to flashpoint, a technique that stood them in good stead once the long fighting retreat back to Germany began.

THE WAR ON the Eastern Front proved to be Germany's nemesis. Following Operation Barbarossa, the German invasion of the Soviet Union in 1941, Germany failed to defeat the Soviet Union and this gave the Soviet leader, Josef Stalin, the breathing space in which to redeploy and rebuild his industrial base and war capability. In 1942, as a consequence, the Red Army counter-attacked and the front rolled inexorably west, finally culminating in the battle for Berlin in 1945 and the end of Hitler's Third Reich. In the mobile battles on the Eastern Front from 1941 to 1944, the Germans deployed panzergrenadiers in large numbers, as the large bodies of armour that were employed on the ideal tank terrain of the open Russian steppe needed infantry support. Panzergrenadiers were in the thick of the action right up to the last desperate battles in Germany and Berlin in 1945.

In these battles panzergrenadiers were employed as motorised infantry, but they also fulfilled many different fighting roles, and were deployed in many different types of terrain. On the Eastern Front, panzergrenadiers fought on the open steppe, in the forests of White Russia, in the ruins of cities such as Stalingrad and Berlin, and in the mountains of the Caucasus. The panzergrenadier was expected to

be flexible and able to adapt to the exigencies of war. This was the case whether fighting in France, the Eastern Front, North Africa or Italy.

Motorisation of Panzergrenadiers

Panzergrenadiers at the beginning of the war were largely lorryborne. It was only as the war on the Eastern Front unfolded that armoured personnel carriers (APCs) replaced lorries and carried the panzergrenadiers into the thick of the action. However, with Allied bombing of Germany's industrial base and major cities, and with major Allied offensives in North Africa, Italy, Normandy and in the Soviet Union, German industry simply could not produce sufficient APCs and armoured fighting vehicles (AFVs) for all the theatres of war in which they were needed. As a consequence, panzergrenadiers often clung onto the sides of panzers (Soviet infantry was carried in a similar fashion on the back of the T-34 Soviet main battle tank), or were carried in whatever lorries were available. The lorries were frequently requisitioned from occupied Europe. Panzergrenadiers were often forced to walk as freezing weather, or petrol and equipment shortages, laid up the available APCs and lorries. The ideal of the mobile panzergrenadier was, by the end of the war, something of a fiction, as panzergrenadiers frequently marched in and out of battle. As the Third Reich collapsed, horses and bicycles were often the only form of 'motorisation' available for many German soldiers.

Left: Armed with rifles and an MP40 machine pistol, members of the Waffen SS in a mixture of dress go 'over the top'. The Waffen SS were used in a 'firefighting' role on the Eastern Front, particularly after 1943, when the Germans were in full retreat.

When the panzergrenadiers went into battle by lorry this affected German tactics. The lorry was a soft-skinned vehicle and provided little or no protection for panzergrenadiers going into action. Thus, instead of the panzergrenadier driving into enemy positions and fighting from the vehicle or debussing at the point of battle, as was possible with an APC, lorry-borne panzergrenadiers would usually debus at a forming-up point following initial contact or a reconnaissance report, after which they would mount a conventional infantry assault. With sufficient APCs, tactics could be adjusted, the panzergrenadier made more mobile and the battle became more dramatic and swift, but this was not always possible. However, whether in APCs or lorries, the panzergrenadier was a vital component to the German attack on the USSR in 1941, for without supporting infantry, the advancing panzers would have been unable to advance so deep into the Soviet Union.

Below: German SS reconnaissance troops mark the direction of their unit's advance on the side of a wrecked Soviet aeroplane during the invasion of Russia. Much of the Soviet air power was destroyed on the ground during Barbarossa.

CASE STUDY ONE: THE ADVANCE ON MOSCOW

SS *Das Reich* Division

In June 1941 the Germans launched Operation Barbarossa, their invasion of the Soviet Union. Later, in the autumn of 1941, the Germans launched Operation Typhoon, the attempt to take Moscow before the Russian winter descended on the combatants. Involved in this operation was *Das Reich* Motorised Division, including the lorryborne *Deutschland* and *Der Führer* Panzer Grenadier regiments. As with the attacks across Meuse in 1940, in 1941 the German armed forces advanced with a mood of optimism borne of continual military success. *Das Reich* Division, part of XL Corps, was attached to Panzer Group 4, and formed part of the spearhead that thrust east up the road to Moscow. *Das Reich* was an elite SS unit, later destroyed when fighting in Normandy in 1944, which, with motorisation and ideological fervour, was the ideal unit to spearhead any attack. This dedication to battle meant that SS units such as *Das Reich* were often brutal in and out of combat. The barbarisation of the war on the Eastern Front led to many

ordinary German soldiers committing appalling atrocities on civilians and Soviet POWs. In this respect, SS units were particularly notorious: following an incident where German POWs were found shot, SS *Leibstandarte Adolf Hitler* panzergrenadiers took no prisoners for several months. All captured Soviet soldiers were shot. This attitude was not restricted to the racial war on the Eastern Front: when *Das Reich* was transferred to France it massacred 642 unarmed villagers at Oradour-sur-Glane in southwest France in reprisal for supposed resistance activity.

Value of motorised infantry

As mentioned earlier, SS units received the best equipment that Germany could produce. In the drive on Moscow in 1941, the APCs available to *Das Reich* were used to good effect: before the autumn rains and winter freeze they gave excellent mobility and flexibility. Everything depended, however, on fuel reaching the overextended front line out on the Russian steppe. It was often the case that fuel shortages, as front-line units awaited their slower logistical train to catch up, meant that units which might advance were forced to await fuel, ammunition and supplies. With

sufficient petrol, APCs and motorcycles gave *Das Reich*'s panzergrenadiers (men would cling on to the motorcycles when the APCs were full) the ability to push forward and seize key points before the Soviets had a chance to mount any defence. The rapidity of motorised infantry also allowed the Germans to seize vital objectives such as bridges before the Soviets could set explosive charges or booby traps. In 1941, the pace was relentless, and the continual need to debus, reconnoitre and sometimes engage, left the panzergrenadiers exhausted, and losses mounted. Having said this, there was the sense of another impending victory, and morale was high. In these operations mobile artillery was vital, and the 37mm Pak mounted on the Sd Kfz 250/10 gave instant support, as did the main armament of the divisional panzers and self-propelled (SP) guns. If anything heavier was needed, the panzergrenadiers had to await the divisional artillery coming up from the rear.

Below: Motorised infantry atop Pz Kpfw III tanks during the battle for Moscow. Fighting directly from tanks was not standard German practice, as troops who chose to do so were exposed to enemy fire and very vulnerable.

Panzergrenadier versus T-34

In the Soviet Union the panzergrenadier also became adept at dealing with the new breed of Soviet armour: the Soviet T-34/76, T-34/85 and heavier SU/KV series. Initially, Soviet tanks proved easy prey for the Germans. However, the T-34, first encountered in 1941, came as a nasty shock: German anti-tank rounds bounced off the T-34's armour and the T-34's main armament proved well able to knock out all the German panzers then available for front-line use. This setback led to the development of the German Panzer V 'Panther' and Panzer VI 'Tiger' tanks, brought into service to counter the T-34, but these were not available in any numbers to the Wehrmacht until 1943. Therefore, panzergrenadiers had to combat the new breed of Soviet tanks with their existing panzers and anti-tank guns, all of which, save the infamous '88', proved inadequate to the task. The panzergrenadiers therefore had to get close enough to the Soviet armour to lay explosive charges. To make this effective, they had to place the explosive charge either in the tracks or in the overhang at the rear of the T-34. Considering that the T-34 was probably moving and was itself supported by Soviet infantry, this was no easy task and required strong nerves and determination.

Panzergrenadiers behind the lines

In the confused fighting of 1941, as the advancing Germans encircled huge numbers of Soviet soldiers, panzergrenadiers were also involved in mopping up operations and protecting lines of communication. This was the fate of the *Grossdeutschland* Division before it went into front-line action. In the forests of White Russia, the men of the *Grossdeutschland* Division were caught up in dense undergrowth as they moved forward to the front. This was warfare akin to the jungles of Burma and, again, proof of the flexibility of the panzergrenadier. The panzergrenadiers would have their nerves stretched to the limit as they moved through dense foliage with visibility down to a few metres. With the confused and fluid fighting in the first few months of the war, hundreds of thousands of Soviet soldiers were trapped behind German lines. Many took the opportunity to surrender; many others, however, resorted to partisan warfare or tried to break out east to reach their own lines. This led to an ongoing battle behind the lines in which panzergrenadiers fought small-scale actions at close quarters, often with knives and bayonets. Snipers were a continual problem as *Grossdeutschland*'s panzergrenadiers attempted to clear wooded areas of

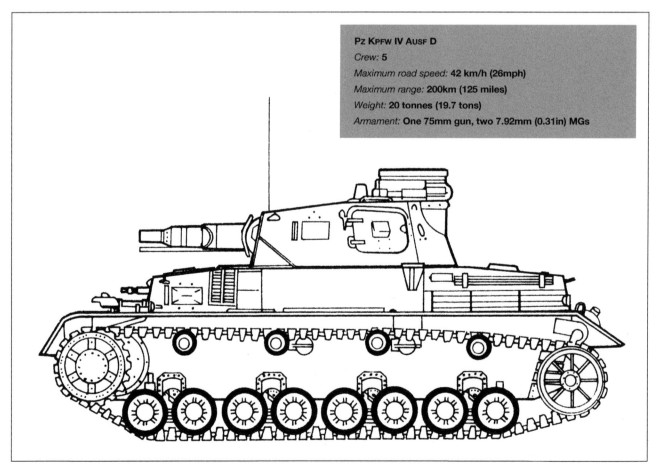

Pz Kpfw IV Ausf D
Crew: **5**
Maximum road speed: **42 km/h (26mph)**
Maximum range: **200km (125 miles)**
Weight: **20 tonnes (19.7 tons)**
Armament: **One 75mm gun, two 7.92mm (0.31in) MGs**

Above: German troops watch as a vehicle burns near a Pz Kpfw III tank during the advance into Russia. Fighting in urban areas required the panzergrenadiers to protect their armour closely, as tanks proved vulnerable when fighting in towns or cities.

trapped Soviet soldiers. These behind-the-lines operations were not classic panzergrenadier warfare, but were almost as important as the front-line duties of a panzergrenadier. The mopping-up operations exhausted panzergrenadiers as each incident required a patrol of tired soldiers to be sent out to try and flush out a sniper or an isolated band of Soviet infantry. The trapped Soviets were particularly adept at night attacks: infiltration would be followed by a shower of hand grenades. The night attacks required alert sentry work and drew upon the reserves of already tired personnel.

Grossdeutschland across the Dnieper

When the *Grossdeutschland* moved into action on the front-line in July 1941 their first task was a river crossing. As at the Meuse crossing in 1940, much of the panzergrenadiers' work was indistinguishable from standard infantry work, except that by being motorised the panzergrenadiers could keep up with the armour. On 11 July the *Grossdeutschland* again effected a river crossing, this time the river Dnieper. Once across the river, on the far bank, a bitter struggle ensued in the vast fields of sunflowers. Small groups of panzergrenadiers fought with the Soviet defenders in the space below the nodding golden flowerheads. The crossing of the Dnieper showed again how panzergrenadiers could lead from the front and clear the way for the panzers' advance. Without the panzergrenadiers, the panzer crews

either had to dismount and force the river themselves or await slower marching infantry coming up from the rear.

Operation Typhoon

In September 1941, as winter approached, Hitler ordered the launch of Operation Typhoon: the final drive to take Moscow. In October, the German panzers and panzergrenadiers began Typhoon. *Das Reich* was given the task of cutting the Smolensk–Moscow highway. When initially involved in the attack, in early October, *Das Reich*'s reconnaissance battalion and motorcycle battalion raced ahead. The remaining panzergrenadiers moved forward as best as they could: some in lorries, some on tanks, some on foot. All along the way, the panzergrenadiers fought a series of confused actions with retreating Soviet infantry, and saw long columns of Soviet POWs heading west into captivity. Because of the fluidity of battle, the distances involved and the rapidity of the German advance, many Soviet soldiers, unwilling to surrender, were trapped behind the German forces and were attempting to escape east back to their own lines. Therefore, panzergrenadiers at or near the front line were often fighting battles both to their front and their rear. Eventually the Germans halted at the gates of Moscow. With winter approaching, temperatures fell, and fell. As winter descended, any battles took place in the few brief hours of daylight remaining each day.

'General Mud' and 'General Winter'

The panzergrenadiers not only encountered resistance from Soviet infantry, but also from the weather and rough terrain. Even moderate rain had the effect of turning the average Russian road into thick mud. This was particularly a problem as there were few metalled roads in the expanses of western Russia on which to maintain the advance. The mud slowed and halted the movement of lorries; even tracked vehicles such as APCs had trouble coping with the thick autumn mud of the Eastern Front.

In these sorts of conditions, the lot of the panzergrenadier was typical of warfare across the ages: mud, rain, cold and a shortage of supplies, along with the ever-present risk of attack. When attacks were mounted, the mud hampered movement and forced panzergrenadiers to hold on to one another just to maintain balance. The autumn rains weighed down their uniforms and sucked the boots from their feet as they attempted to march east. The mud needed to harden for effective mobile operations. The problem was that when this happened the mud was replaced by the freezing Russian winter that would halt operations as the thermometer fell below -40°C.

Below: The coming of autumn brought heavy rains and thick mud on the Eastern Front, and the ground would be equally bad after the winter freeze had thawed – far from ideal conditions for rapid, motorised movement.

The Russian winter was an unforgettable experience for the panzergrenadier, and proved to be as great an enemy in 1941 as the Soviet army in defence of Moscow. The panzergrenadiers' APCs and lorries, designed for European operations, were simply not built for such extremes. The slicing winds and freezing cold made the track and firing pins brittle and liable to snap; hydraulic fluid froze in gun recoil buffers, rendering the gun useless; ammunition refused to fire and the breechblocks of rifles froze solid. Oil congealed to the consistency of treacle and engines had to be kept running, using up precious fuel. The drag on dynamos made starting engines impossible, battery plates became warped, engine cylinder blocks split open, and axles refused to turn.

The panzergrenadiers were woefully unprepared. Only grenades functioned properly in the Russian winter. To add to the cold and frostbite, many panzergrenadiers had dysentery and were forced to perform bodily functions in the open. Everyday chores became impossible. If a man drawing his ration of boiling soup at the field kitchen could not find his spoon, it would be lukewarm in 30 seconds. Any further delay risked the soup turning cold and then freezing solid.

Above: Panzergrenadiers advancing to contact in halftracks at the battle of Kursk, 1943, the largest tank battle to date. Panzergrenadiers played a significant role in clearing the extensive Soviet defences built up around the salient.

During November 1941, the mud froze as temperatures and snow fell. While this allowed mobile operations, the German soldiers of Army Group Centre pushing on Moscow were unprepared for the approaching Russian winter, since the German High Command expected the war to have been won by October 1941. The winter equipment for the German panzergrenadier in Russia was still in Poland, and had not been sent forward for fear of blocking supply lines just as the German offensive was underway. As a consequence, over his standard uniform the German soldier had only his denim overalls, padded with newspaper to resist the cold. The lack of shelter intensified the cold. The ground was frozen and so impossible for digging (except with dynamite), and local buildings had been destroyed in the fighting or burned by the retreating Soviet troops. By mid-November, many panzergrenadier units had over 50 percent frostbite casualties. Therefore, when the Soviets launched any counter-attacks, panzergrenadiers were short of effectives as men were hospitalised with frostbite. The panzergrenadiers also discovered that their automatic weapons were so frozen that they could only fire single shots. The freezing temperatures made a mockery of mobile warfare, as vehicles were laid up and unable to move in the freezing conditions. Gunners found that the packing grease for their shells had frozen and had to be scraped off with a knife before being loaded into the gun breech. Meanwhile, Soviet infantry,

accustomed to the cold and in quilted jackets, attacked with the support of ever increasing numbers of T-34 tanks, against which the standard German 37mm anti-tank gun was useless at anything but point-blank range.

General Heinz Guderian, commanding 2nd Panzer Group, wrote to his wife on 28 November: 'Only he who saw the endless expanse of Russian snow during this winter of our misery, and felt the icy wind that blew across it, burying in snow every object in its path; who drove for hour after hour through that no man's land only at last to find too thin shelter, with insufficiently clothed half-starved men; and who also saw by contrast the well-fed, warmly clad and fresh Siberians, fully equipped for winter fighting; only a man who knew all that can truly judge the events which now occurred.' Yet Operation Typhoon continued, with the Germans maintaining the attempt to take Moscow.

In early December 1941, the Soviets, led by Marshal Georgi Zhukov launched a full-scale counter-attack and pushed the Germans back to the start line for Operation Typhoon. This counter-offensive destroyed many German units and ended any chance of a quick victory. It also

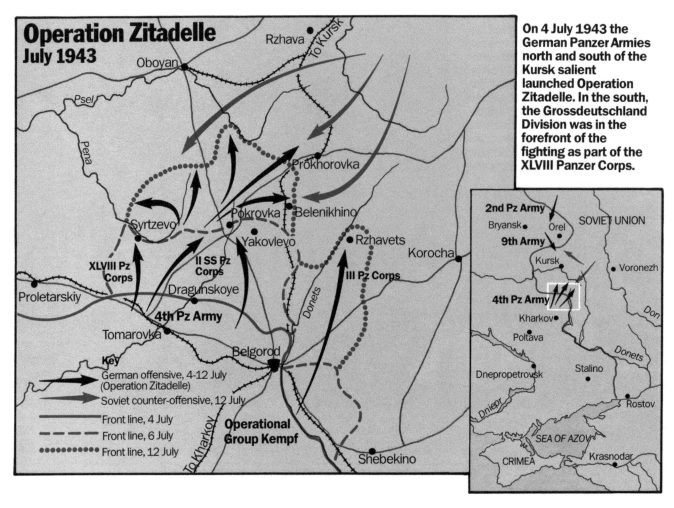

Operation Zitadelle
July 1943

On 4 July 1943 the German Panzer Armies north and south of the Kursk salient launched Operation Zitadelle. In the south, the Grossdeutschland Division was in the forefront of the fighting as part of the XLVIII Panzer Corps.

Key
German offensive, 4-12 July (Operation Zitadelle)
Soviet counter-offensive, 12 July
Front line, 4 July
Front line, 6 July
Front line, 12 July

smashed many of the panzergrenadier units involved in the push on Moscow. By the end of the attack, the 1st Battalion of Infantry Regiment *Grossdeutschland* had been reduced to a company. All along the German line, depleted, frost-bitten panzergrenadier units retreated, and the chance to capture Moscow evaporated. The winter of 1941 would be a period of rebuilding for the panzergrenadier before Hitler's 1942 offensive: a push across southern Russia with the objective of capturing Stalingrad and the oilfields of Baku.

Summary

What does the push on Moscow tell the historian about the role of the panzergrenadier? Firstly, Operation Barbarossa would have been impossible without infantry that could keep up with the armour. Secondly, the panzergrenadier was involved behind the lines as well as in the front line. Thirdly, while panzergrenadiers were often reduced to marching, the presence of APCs, lorries and motorcycles was sufficient to give panzergrenadiers the edge to race ahead, frequently ahead of the panzers, to reconnoitre, protect vital points and, if necessary, attack. Fourthly, this

was an all-arms endeavour: panzers, dive-bombers, combat engineers and self-propelled guns worked alongside the panzergrenadiers. Fifthly, anti-partisan operations and river crossings show how the panzergrenadier could be called upon for a variety of tasks that extended beyond the traditional role of armoured infantry support.

Finally, any success by the panzergrenadiers has to be measured against the Germans' lack of preparation for the Russian weather. Mud and cold halted and defeated the panzergrenadiers as much as Soviet resistance. This lack of preparation shows the importance of measuring the panzergrenadiers' success at the local level in the light of deficient overall German grand strategy.

CASE STUDY TWO:
THE BATTLE OF KURSK, 1943

The euphoria of the initial advance on Moscow had changed by 1943, especially following the battle of Stalingrad in 1942–43 where the German Sixth Army had been encircled and defeated. In the summer of 1943, the Germans launched their major offensive for the year by attacking the Soviet lines around the city of Kursk. The code name for the offensive was Operation Citadelle (or 'Zitadelle'). The 1942–43 winter campaign had left a westward bulge 118 miles wide and 75 miles deep in the front around Kursk, an important rail junction some 500 miles to the south of Moscow. The battle of Kursk called for converging attacks by two German armies against the northern and southern flanks of the Soviet bulge with the aim of nipping out the salient, capturing or destroying the Soviet forces involved, and using the victory as a springboard for future attacks. The battle involved employing the bulk of the panzer/panzergrenadier armies so painstakingly built up following the defeat at the battle of Stalingrad.

Heinz Guderian

In February 1943, Guderian had been brought in to take over the Eastern Front. Reinstated as Inspector General of Armoured Troops, Guderian looked to build fully equipped tank divisions, rather than a number of partially equipped ones. For 1944 he was trying to create divisions capable of large scale operations, each equipped with 400 tanks and a balanced mix of supporting arms. Far better, he urged, to have only a few hard hitting divisions than many weak ones. The aim, ultimately, was to have large panzer armies (or *panzerwaffe*) capable of taking on the Soviet tank armies being equipped from the Soviet factories that had been relocated in 1941 to safety east of the Ural mountains. Panzergrenadiers formed a crucial element of these new tank armies.

Guderian was not keen on the Kursk operation, preferring to wait for an attack in 1944. The problem was that Hitler ignored Guderian's worries about the irreplaceable losses in men and tanks an offensive in 1943 would cause, and agreed Operation Citadelle to attack Kursk. Hitler then interfered further by insisting on more of the latest Panther and Tiger tanks for the operation. This led to delays in the date for the attack. Hitler's decision was the worst of both worlds and compounded the German situation. By July 1943, the month Kursk would be launched, the Germans'

Below: German armour – tanks, armoured personnel carriers, and assault guns – advance in formation across the Russian steppe during Operation *Zitadelle*, the battle for the Kursk salient, which saw large numbers of casualties on both sides.

Above: A StuG III and lorryborne infantry from a German panzergrenadier division advance past knocked-out Russian T-34s. The panzergrenadiers would debus from their lorries some distance away from the front line itself.

delay meant that they had lost the element of surprise and were attacking over heavily fortified ground of the enemy's choosing, and on which there was little room to manoeuvre. This delay shows the importance of measuring the skill at arms of the individual panzergrenadier against a flawed German grand strategy.

Kursk: the clash of armour

The battle of Kursk was certainly unique, and was the toughest single battle for the panzergrenadier on the Eastern Front. Kursk was also the biggest tank battle in history with over 6000 tanks and self-propelled guns involved. By contrast, the battle of El Alamein in North Africa in 1942 involved around 1500 tanks; later battles such as the battle of 'Chinese Farm' in the 1973 Arab–Israeli War in the Sinai in 1973 saw some 2000 tanks deployed. Kursk is also rightly regarded as the greatest tank battle in history, and is seen as the swan song of the German armoured forces. In all, some 900,000 Germans with 2,700 fighting vehicles assembled for the battle of Kursk.

To push into entrenched Soviet positions involved the panzergrenadier working in combination with the panzers, artillery and air support. The problem was that the new breed of panzers built to take on the T-34 were not ready for battle. For instance, the Panzer V 'Panther' had not been

thoroughly tested before its debut at Kursk. The roads and tracks between the railheads and the assembly areas for Kursk were soon littered with Panthers that had broken down with transmission failures and engine fires. Guderian was well aware that Hitler was rushing the Panthers into action too early, and before they had been fully 'worked up' on the training grounds. Guderian's appraisal before Kursk was that 'the Panthers, on whose performance the Chief of the Army General Staff was relying so heavily, were still suffering from many teething troubles inherent in all new equipment and it seemed unlikely that these could all be put right in time for the launching of the attack.' Thus, the panzergrenadiers at Kursk would be handicapped by having to go into battle alone, as their armoured support was knocked out or, more likely, had broken down.

The Soviet defences at Kursk

The panzergrenadier would also be facing formidable Soviet defences. The delay caused by Hitler's obsession with controlling operations gave the Soviets added time to transform the Kursk salient into an impregnable fortress. This they did with speed and completeness. The Russians constructed six interlocking defensive belts to a depth of 25 miles with covering belts of trenches, strongpoints and barbed wire. Supporting these defences in depth were 20,000 guns, of which one-third were anti-tank weapons. Simultaneously, the Russians laid minefields, to a density of 2500 anti-personnel and 2200 anti-tank mines per mile of front. In all, 400,000 mines were laid; streams were dammed to make impassable flooded areas and otherwise rich, fertile farmland was turned into a gigantic obstacle course for the attacking Germans. The Soviet High Command (or Stavka) pressed local Russian civilians into digging 3000 miles of defensive trenches, carefully criss-crossed to allow mobility for the Russian infantry; artillery, anti-tank and machine-gun nests were sited to provide mutual support and create a 'curtain of fire' with which to meet the German attack. It would be these defences that the panzergrenadier would have to storm.

Backing up these defences, the Russians amassed a huge force of fighters and bombers, and the biggest tank force ever. Into the bulge at Kursk the Russians crammed seven armies. Meanwhile, reserve forces of a tank army and two infantry armies were concentrated 150 miles behind the front. The reserve armies built additional defensive belts in front of their positions. When all the preparations were complete, 1,336,000 men, 3444 tanks, 2900 aircraft and 19,000 guns were ready for the battle of Kursk. As much as 75 per cent of all Russian armour was now located in and around Kursk.

On 5 July 1943, Hermann Hoth's Fourth Panzer Army of 18 divisions (10 armoured) attacked from the south of Kursk, while simultaneously Walther Model's Ninth Army, also of 18 divisions (7 armoured) attacked in the north. In all, some 20 panzer/panzergrenadier divisions gathered at Kursk for the panzergrenadiers' biggest battle.

Panzergrenadiers at Kursk: *Grossdeutschland*

As at the Meuse crossing in 1940, combat engineers were the first into action. Even before the panzergrenadiers and panzers moved forward, combat engineers worked in no-man's land clearing a way through the dense Soviet minefields. So thickly were these sown that one ten-man *Grossdeutschland* team under Oberleutnant Balletshofer lifted 2700 mines in one night's hard work. At 0500 hours on 5 July the German artillery opened up, the battle of Kursk had begun. The barrage on both sides of the salient expended more shells than the whole of the Polish and French campaigns combined. The panzergrenadiers then went into action with the panzers. However, the Soviet defence was so fierce that the panzergrenadiers were effectively functioning as infantry, as the panzers soon bogged down. The minefields and the Soviet defences outlined above halted the panzers in their tracks and left the grenadiers bereft of armoured support. The Germans failed to penetrate the Soviets' second line of defence and the panzergrenadiers settled down to a fierce slog against determined resistance.

As always, it was the combination of the motorised infantry in an all-arms endeavour with tank, artillery and air

A sergeant in the *Grossdeutschland* Panzergrenadier Division, the premier infantry unit of the Wehrmacht, shown here at the time of the Kursk offensive in July 1943. He is a member of the assault gun detachment, who provided direct fire support for the panzergrenadiers as they fought through the complex Russian defence systems.

support that would carry the day. The problem was that the tanks became bogged down in the intricate Soviet defences. The dense minefields also proved a deadly opponent. APCs and observation armoured cars were destroyed; those tanks not bogged down had tracks blown off. As the official history of the *Grossdeutschland* recalls: 'The Panzer Regiment GD and the Panther brigade were supposed to attack...however they had the misfortune to drive into a minefield which had escaped notice until then – and this even before reaching the bolshevik trenches! It was enough to make one sick. Soldiers and officers alike feared that the entire affair was going to pot. The tanks were stuck fast, some bogged down to the tops of their tracks, and to make matters worse the enemy was firing at them with anti-tank rifles, anti-tank guns and artillery. Tremendous confusion breaks out. The fusiliers advance without the tanks – what can they do? The tanks do not follow. Scarcely does the enemy notice the precarious situation of the fusiliers when he launches a counter-attack supported by numerous close support aircraft. The infantry companies of III Panzer-Fusilier regiment GD...walked straight into ruin. Even the heavy company suffered 50 killed and wounded in a few hours. Pioneers were moved up immediately and they began to clear a path through the mine-infested terrain. Ten more hours had to pass before the first tanks and

self-propelled guns got through and reached the infantry.' This quote shows how panzergrenadiers at Kursk, as at the Meuse in 1940, frequently led from the front.

The attritional battle

On both the northern and southern sectors, tanks, SP guns and panzergrenadiers crawled forward in the face of fierce resistance. This was not the mobile warfare of the advance on Moscow of 1941 or the drive to the Caucasus in 1942. Each obstacle cleared revealed another defensive position. Assault pioneers were in constant demand to clear the minefields. Once through the minefields the panzers moved forward with accompanying grenadiers to the next minefield. The ever-present risk of ambush meant that panzergrenadier support was vital to stop Soviet tank-busting infantry teams from moving in and knocking out the panzers at close range with explosive charges. The defence-in-depth of the Soviet lines was formidable. Deep excavated bunkers with built in flame-throwers had to be knocked out one-by-one. Dug in and camouflaged T-34s provided fire support. The panzergrenadiers and engineers had to clear these defences before the panzers could move forward and break out behind the enemy lines. Casualties mounted. Once into the enemy lines the panzergrenadier would establish all-round 'hedgehog' defences with the remaining panzers and

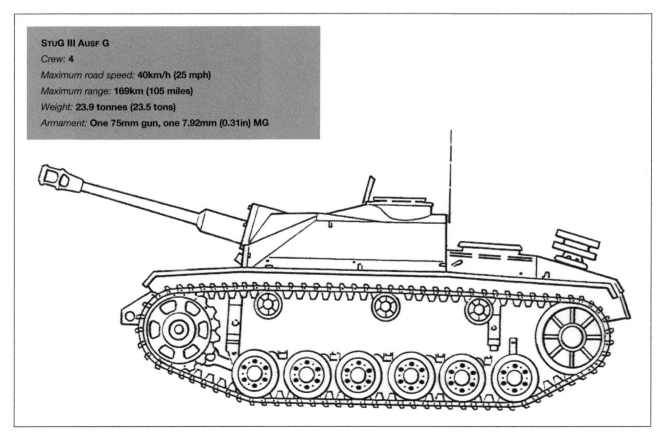

STUG III AUSF G
Crew: **4**
Maximum road speed: **40km/h (25 mph)**
Maximum range: **169km (105 miles)**
Weight: **23.9 tonnes (23.5 tons)**
Armament: **One 75mm gun, one 7.92mm (0.31in) MG**

settle in for the night. To unsettle the Germans and prevent sleep, Soviet light aircraft patrolled the lines at night dropping anti-personnel bombs on any visible fires in the enemy lines. Soviet rockets, the famous Katyushas, pounded the German defences. Set in the back of a truck, each Katyusha launcher could send a salvo of four tons of explosives over an area of ten acres. The panzergrenadiers feared these rockets more than the artillery. There was no familiar rush of sound, and once released the rockets distributed their load randomly and with great force.

Instead of breaking through the Soviet lines, the German forces were merely sitting in the middle of the enemy defences with little hope of breaking through. All the while, breakdowns, mines and Soviet guns took their toll of the APCs and panzers. This was a far cry from the heady days of September 1939 or May 1940.

Summary

The battle of Kursk was a defeat for the Germans and drained the strength of the German armed forces. The panzergrenadier at Kursk was fighting a new type of battle: one more akin to a World War I Western Front battle such as Passchendaele or Verdun, albeit with armoured support. This was another example of the flexibility of the panzergrenadier, but Kursk was not a battle where the panzergrenadier could show off his dash and mobility. Kursk turned out to be an attritional slog through formidable defences that confounded the Germans.

CASE STUDY THREE:
THE BATTLE FOR GERMANY, 1944–45

By 1944, panzergrenadiers on the Eastern Front were fighting the type of warfare carried out by the *Hitler Jugend* Division in Normandy. Germany was now on the defensive and the motorised infantry was now primarily deployed in a defensive role. Panzergrenadiers would still launch local counter-attacks but the main task now was to delay the Allied offensives from west, east and south – panzergrenadiers also fought in the Italian campaign – closing in on Germany.

Panzergrenadier versus Soviet 150mm howitzer

Across the front line in the east, panzergrenadiers prepared for the Soviet assault. Panzergrenadiers launched local counter-attacks, as in the areas of the Baltic republics not yet taken by the Soviets. In one such attack, a platoon leader's APC was advancing at speed on the road to the town of Kursenei. As the halftrack rolled around a hidden bend in the

Above: Panzergrenadiers clearing out defenders from a fortified farmhouse on the Eastern Front. The panzergrenadiers were regularly called upon to perform such tasks, to remove any potential risk to the precious German tanks.

road, the APC and its occupants found itself looking down the barrel of a 150mm Soviet howitzer, a few metres from the APC. There was nothing to do but get out and storm the gun. As the panzergrenadiers poured out of the APC, the half-track began reversing back around the bend. Soviet infantry in the woods engaged the attacking panzergrenadiers, wounding several before Unteroffizier Röger leaped onto the running board of the gun tractor and emptied his sub-machine gun into the driver's cab. The rest of the Soviet gun crew chased Röger under the gun carriage, but before they could deal with him, German reinforcements arrived. For this and other brave deeds, Röger received the Knight's Cross at the end of August 1944.

The battle for the Seelow Heights and Germany, 1945

Panzergrenadiers were also in the thick of the action in the final desperate German efforts to prevent the fall of Berlin. During mid April 1945 they fought to contain the Soviet armour that had broken through the German defences to advance across the Seelow Heights to Berlin. The battle of the Seelow Heights opened on 16 April, when Russian searchlights illuminated the German positions for a pre-dawn attack. Artillery and fighter-bombers pounded the

Germans in preparation for the assault. As the Soviet tanks moved forward there was mayhem, as tanks and infantry were caught by the determined German defence. Even at this late stage of the war, when defeat was almost inevitable, the panzergrenadier still fought with fanatical determination. After heavy fighting, the Russians forced the Germans off the Seelow Heights and advanced on Berlin.

Brandenburg panzergrenadiers

The defence offered by the German Panzer Grenadier Division *Brandenburg* to the Soviet assault gives some idea of the type of fighting at the battle of the Seelow Heights. The Brandenburgers were originally a special forces unit that increased to a divisional-sized panzergrenadier division and worked in conjunction with the *Grossdeutschland* Division. As special forces, the Brandenburgers adapted to the life of a panzergrenadier and became one of Germany's

Below: Panzergrenadiers break off from the main advance to neutralise a defended Russian hamlet, whilst the tanks bypass the defences either side. The panzergrenadiers would debus out of the defender's line of fire but their speed of movement into combat gave them a decisive advantage.

premier fighting units. In the last days of the war on the Eastern Front, the Brandenburg panzergrenadiers were quickly involved in ferocious fighting as they attempted to stem the Russian onrush. These were the last days of the Reich, but this only stiffened the German defenders' resolve. The Russians soon had their armour across the Oder and Neisse rivers, but in the town of Kaltwasser the Brandenburgers made a stand. As at Stalingrad, tanks were at a disadvantage in urban warfare, and using Panzerfausts the Germans quickly knocked out a number of the T-34s. In towns like Kaltwasser the panzergrenadiers fought vigorous rearguard actions with little armoured support. Tank-busting teams of panzergrenadiers used Panzerfausts and explosive charges to take on the T-34s and JS tanks at close range. The T-34s were accompanied in built-up areas by teams of Russian infantry, so the German infantry had to contend with holding off the infantry while grenadier squads moved in to lay hollow explosive charges that could disable the Russian armour. Frequently, the only weapon available was the 'Molotov cocktail' petrol bomb that could set a T-34 ablaze with a good shot. In the end, however, the panzergrenadiers were outnumbered and they fell back to fight a last desperate defence of the German capital.

Above: An SS panzergrenadier section in camouflage blouses advance through a wood in Eastern Prussia in late 1944. By this stage of the war the panzergrenadiers were moved rapidly between sections of the front to try to stem the Soviet advance.

The battle for Berlin

The attack into Germany involved not just breaking the German lines centred on the Seelow Heights in front of Berlin, but advancing into a built-up area encompassing hundreds of square miles of buildings, roads, sewers, tunnels and railways. As was proved at Stalingrad, tanks were very vulnerable in city fighting, where determined grenadiers fighting as conventional infantry could hold up an armoured advance using roofs, windows and sewers to enfilade the tanks with petrol bombs, mines and Panzerfausts. At close ranges, and in the deadly environment of close-quarter fighting in built-up areas like Berlin, the Russians needed to be wary.

The battle for Berlin was going to be one of the hardest fought battles of the Eastern Front. By late April 1945, the Germans had been pushed back into the suburbs and the centre of Berlin itself. Pounded by Allied air forces during the war, the Russians now added to the destruction as they advanced into the city with heavy artillery barrages. The rubble, however, provided excellent defensive positions from which small, isolated German units held out.

To overcome the German defences inside Berlin, Russian tanks often took the expedient of driving through the buildings to avoid exposing themselves to the German infantry waiting in the rubble of the streets. Civilian casualties were heavy as the Russians applied overwhelming firepower to their advance. Office and apartment blocks came crashing down as the Russians pushed on towards the Reichstag and German Chancellory. By 27 April, the Russians had reached Potsdamer Platz, just a few hundred yards from Hitler's bunker. The last days of the Third Reich witnessed the last battle for the panzergrenadier.

Summary: the panzergrenadiers' last stand

The battle for Berlin saw the panzergrenadiers dismounted and fighting as conventional infantry. While understrength, the SS Panzer Grenadier Division *Nordland*, the SS *Polizei* Division, the 18th Panzer Grenadier Division, the 20th Panzer Grenadier Division and the 25th Panzer Grenadier Division were all involved in the final battle in the ruins of Berlin in April–May 1945. There were also foreign volunteer SS panzergrenadiers in the city. The few panzers available allowed local counter-attacks. On 2 May 1945, in one of the last actions of the war in Europe, the 11th SS Volunteer Panzer Grenadier Division *Nordland*'s last two Panther tanks spearheaded an attempt by the remnants of the encircled Berlin garrison to escape Soviet captivity. Even though both tanks were destroyed, they helped create a tiny gap in the Soviet encirclement that allowed several hundred troops of the garrison to fight their way out west to surrender to the Americans. Many panzergrenadiers on the Eastern Front tried to follow their example, but not all made it.

CHAPTER 5

The Firepower
of a Panzergrenadier

HEINZ GUDERIAN CONSIDERED that the three key factors to the successful prosecution of armoured warfare were protection, mobility and firepower. For the panzergrenadier, the Sd Kfz 251 provided the first and, importantly, the second of these factors. However, Guderian considered that the most important factor of the three was firepower. Thus it was central to the effectiveness of Germany's panzer arm that its elite mobile infantry component was correspondingly well armed. As the panzergrenadiers were required to fight a variety of actions – support of the armour on the offensive, standard infantry attacks, assaults on fortified positions that the tanks could not tackle and defensive actions either as infantry alone or in combination with the armour – they required a wide range of weaponry. This is particularly true in the case of the panzergrenadier division because, traditionally, the division is the smallest formation in which all arms are combined, and it contained infantry, armour, anti-aircraft guns and artillery. Nonetheless, it should be remembered that, although usually more lavishly equipped than much of the remainder of the Wehrmacht, particularly in the case of the Waffen SS, very little of the panzergrenadiers' weaponry was exclusive to them. However, to understand their tactics and performance in battle a survey of some of the more common weapons

Essential to the panzergrenadier's ability to fight was his ability to hit the enemy hard, and quickly. Panzergrenadiers, like their regular German infantry counterparts, were heavily-armed with pistols, grenades, rifles, machine guns, flamethrowers, panzerfausts, and a host of other weaponry.

with which the panzergrenadiers fought is useful. This list is not comprehensive, given the bewildering variety of equipment used by the Germans in World War II, but covers a representative selection of the more common arms of the panzergrenadiers.

SMALL ARMS

Pistols

Handguns are of very limited use in modern warfare. They are comparatively inaccurate, and even in the hands of a marksman are rarely effective over ranges of 40 or 50 metres and, except at close range, of little lethality due to their small calibre. Furthermore, for such a small weapon the pistol takes up considerable industrial potential and skill to manufacture. Traditionally it was also a weapon for officers and senior non-commissioned officers. Thus the carrier of a handgun was easily identified as such and a prime target for snipers. During World War I, officers soon took to carrying rifles, which quite apart from being more effective weapons, rendered them almost indistinguishable from their men. Nonetheless, handguns were issued in their hundreds of thousands in World War II and for the German armed forces demand always exceeded supply. This was because, despite the reasons listed above, the pistol continued to play an important role. For many troops, carrying a larger personal weapon such as a rifle was out of the question. In the cramped confines of a vehicle there was little space to stow anything other than a pistol, yet should the crew be forced

Left: A *Grossdeutschland* flamethrower team in action during the summer of 1942 on the Eastern Front. The flamethrower was a fearsome weapon, but it proved extremely useful for clearing bunkers and emplacements.

to leave the vehicle in combat they required some sort of weapon for self-defence. This was of considerable relevance to highly motorised units such as the panzergrenadiers. It should also be remembered that in close-quarter combat such as trench clearance and urban warfare, possessing a handy and easily aimed weapon is of great benefit.

The German Army had adopted the semi-automatic pistol in favour of the revolver early in the twentieth century; therefore, unlike many other armies, the revolver had an almost minimal presence in the Wehrmacht. The famous Pistole P 08, more widely known as the Luger, was adopted as the German service pistol in 1908 and served throughout World War I. It was extremely popular with the troops as it was easy to handle and aim, and usually extremely well made. Nonetheless, it was not ideally suited to trench warfare. Its complicated upward opening toggle lock mechanism was prone to clog with dirt and mud. The Luger thus required considerable care and maintenance. It was also complicated and slow to manufacture. The Walther P 38 (see below) replaced it as the German service pistol in 1938. However, the Luger continued in parallel production with the Walther until 1942 and gave sterling service throughout World War II.

■ Pistole P 08

CARTRIDGE: 9mm Parabellum; WEIGHT (all weights given empty): 0.877kg (1.93lb); MAGAZINE CAPACITY: 8 round box

Popular as the Luger was, it was not compatible with the increased military production volume required by the German war machine. Therefore, Walther Waffenfabrik produced the excellent P 38 in response to the need for a more simply manufactured weapon. Most of the first production models went to the panzer arm. The P 38 incorporated some excellent safety features, such as a double action trigger which allowed the pistol to be carried securely with the safety catch off. Most importantly it was robust and well liked by the troops. This was because the pistol sat well in the hand and had a crisp, clean trigger action, all of which enhanced its accuracy. The Walther action also kept out the dirt and dust. Perhaps most importantly, it continued to function in the extremes of climate on the Eastern Front. Indeed, as temperatures dropped to such low levels that gun oil froze, the pistol could be kept free of oil and continue to function.

There were never enough of either the P 08 or P 38 available and the Germans pressed into use all sorts of pistols from a variety of manufacturers. The Walther PP

The recommended method from the training manual for dealing with defenders in trenches with bayonet fixed.

The recommended method from the training manual for using the butt of the rifle in hand-to-hand combat.

Above: German infantry practice hand-to-hand combat with the Gewehr 98k rifle. Although based on a World War I design, the rifle was a good, sturdy weapon, and equipped many thousands of panzergrenadiers throughout the war.

and PPK, and various Sauer, Steyr and Mauser models also saw service. The famous Mauser C/96 'Broomhandle' pistol was used by the Waffen SS, but even in its automatic 'Schnellfeuer' form the C/96 was a somewhat dated and clumsy weapon. The arsenals of many of the nations conquered by the Reich were plundered to equip the Wehrmacht. Amongst the better foreign pistols used by the Germans were the 9mm Polish Radom wz.35, known in German service as the Pistole P 35(p) and the 9mm Belgium Browning Highpower, called by the Germans the Pistole P 620(b). Both were kept in production throughout the war, their output almost entirely going to the SS.

■ **Walther P 38**
CARTRIDGE: 9mm Parabellum; WEIGHT: 0.960kg (2.15lb)
MAGAZINE CAPACITY: 8 round box

Submachine-Guns

Easier to handle than a rifle, capable of producing large volumes of automatic fire and relatively compact, the submachine-gun, termed the machine pistol by the Germans, reigned supreme in close-quarter fighting. Within panzergrenadier formations, officers, NCOs, special assault

squads and specialists were equipped with machine pistols. Also, most large combat vehicles had enough space for at least one such weapon. Waffen SS formations were the largest user of the Bergman MP 35, which was a direct descendant of the World War I Bergman MP 18. Manufactured to an extremely high standard, with walnut furniture, these were excellent weapons, but the MP 35 was a product of a different age and too difficult to mass-produce in the numbers required, although it was made until 1945.

The MP 38, the most famous German submachine-gun of the war, was something very different indeed. While not particularly innovative as a gun, it was revolutionary in terms of the mass production methods used in its manufacture. The MP 38 was constructed from metal stampings, die cast parts and plastic furniture; it was simple but also robust and effective. Its compactness made it ideal for troops carried in the cramped confines of a vehicle such as the Sd Kfz 251 and was a popular weapon with the panzergrenadiers, who received priority in its allocation. Its manufacture was further simplified in 1940 and the resulting weapon was known as the MP 40. To the troops who rightly prized this reliable and handy weapon this change would have made little noticeable difference. Incidentally, the MP38/MP 40's nickname the 'Schmeisser' is something of a misnomer, since Hugo Schmeisser had nothing to do with the Erma-designed weapon.

■ **MP 40**
CALIBRE: 9mm Parabellum; WEIGHT: 4kg (8.8lb); MAGAZINE CAPACITY: 32 round box; CYCLIC RATE OF FIRE: 500rpm

The Germans also used vast quantities of captured Soviet PPSh-41s; many were even chambered to allow their own 9mm ammunition to be used.

Rifles

Despite the popularity and usefulness of the MP 40, most panzergrenadiers would have been equipped with the Mauser-designed Karabiner 98k, although the older, less handy World War I veteran, the Gewehr 98, often saw service too. Perhaps, on the vast steppes of Russia this was an advantage, for the 7.92mm bolt-action 98k was accurate to a 1000 metres. They were sturdy, reliable rifles, used in every campaign of the war. If the 98k had a failing, it was its five round magazine capacity, compared with the ten rounds of the British Lee Enfield or eight of the American Garand M1.

■ **Karabiner 98k**
CALIBRE: 7.92mm; WEIGHT: 3.9kg (8.6lb); LENGTH: 1.1075m (3.38ft); MAGAZINE CAPACITY: 5 round box

All the armies of the major participants in World War II, with the exception of the United States, went to war with bolt-action rifles as the main personal weapon of their infantry. Yet by 1940 the Wehrmacht had identified the need for a self-loading rifle to increase the firepower of the troops. The experience of facing the Soviet SVT40 rifle on the Eastern Front – the Wehrmacht used as many of these rifles as they could get their hands on – reinforced this conclusion. Walther came up with the 7.92mm Gewehr 41(W) which proved difficult to produce, overly heavy and difficult to load. Nonetheless, as the only self-loading rifle the Germans had, it saw extensive service on the Eastern Front. Learning from the SVT40, the gas operation of which Walther copied almost in its entirety, they produced the improved Gewehr 43. The Gewehr 43 was a more practical combat design and due to the retention of the powerful 7.92mm rifle cartridge made an excellent sniper rifle.

■ Gewehr 43
CALIBRE: 7.92mm; WEIGHT: 4.4kg (9.7lb); LENGTH: 1.117m (3.4ft); MAGAZINE CAPACITY: 10 round box

The Gewehr 43, although a useful weapon, did not make a particularly large impact on weapon design. The SVT40 and Garand M1 were easily better rifles. The StG 44, however,

Above: SS panzergrenadiers clean their weapons whilst recuperating in France in 1942. German small arms were extremely well designed on the whole, and if kept clean would perform reliably in combat conditions.

was one of the most influential firearms of the war, as it was the first modern assault rifle. German after-action studies came to the conclusion that most infantry combat took place under ranges of 400 metres. However, the German soldier was carrying a rifle that was accurate above 1000 metres. The infantry would be better armed with something that combined the firepower and handiness of a sub-machine gun in the assault and could fire accurate selective fire in defence. Early experiments using the 7.92mm rifle cartridge proved a failure, as such powerful ammunition was too much of a handful when fired on automatic.

The Haenel team under Louis Schmeisser, however, developed the Maschinenkarbiner 42(H), which fired a new kurz (short) 7.92mm cartridge that, though it resembled the equivalent rifle round, was shortened and contained less propellant. It lacked the range of the traditional cartridge but at most combat ranges up to 600 metres was more than adequate; importantly it could be comfortably handled during automatic fire. Trials were undertaken on the Eastern Front where it was initially known as the *Maschinenpistole* 43 or MP 43 to disguise it from Hitler's notice, as he disapproved of the assault rifle programme. The troops waxed lyrical about the new weapon and its reputation was sealed when, according to legend, a batch of the new rifles was dropped to a German unit surrounded by Soviet formations. Using the MP 43 they proceeded to fight their way out of the encirclement. Eventually, such was demand for the new weapon by the army, Hitler relented and bestowed on it a more suitable name, the *Sturmgewehr* (assault rifle) 44 or StG 44.

The StG 44 represented a quantum leap in an individual infantryman's firepower compared with his bolt-action rifle-armed counterpart. It revolutionised infantry tactics, making a squad far less dependent on supporting fire from heavy machine guns, as they carried their own fire support with them. The rifle was highly sought-after and, despite its ease of manufacture, only went to elite front-line units such as the Waffen SS and panzergrenadiers. Even within such formations its distribution was limited. In a 'typical' Type 1945 panzer division only a single specialist *sturm* (assault) platoon in each company would be equipped with the StG 44.

■ **StG 44**
Calibre: 7.92mm (kurz); Weight: 5.22kg (11.5lb); Length: 940mm; Cyclic Rate of Fire: 500rpm; Magazine: 30 round box

Machine Guns

Central to all German infantry tactics was the squad's light machine-gun, particularly panzergrenadier formations. In *Achtung–Panzer!* Guderian explained that: 'They need to put down a heavy volume of fire, and require a correspondingly large complement of machine-guns and ammunition.' Indeed, a motorised or panzergrenadier division contained as many as 1101 machine-guns. An infantry division had only 643 (although this rose to 656 in 1944). Although many armies retained their World War I heavy machine-guns (the ageing German MG 08 saw extensive service), most had a separate light machine-gun design such as the British Bren or American BAR as the squad support weapon. In the mid 1930s the Germans developed the new concept of the general purpose machine-gun by producing a gun that was light enough to be carried by one man and used in the assault role, but when mounted on a tripod could produce the volume of fire of a heavy machine-gun. This was the Rheinmetall *Maschinengewehr* 34 or MG 34,

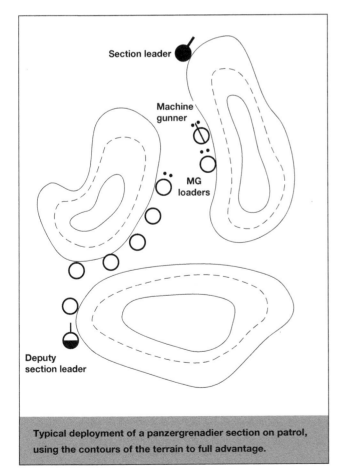

Typical deployment of a panzergrenadier section on patrol, using the contours of the terrain to full advantage.

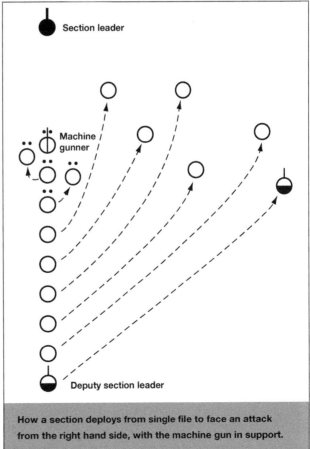

How a section deploys from single file to face an attack from the right hand side, with the machine gun in support.

Above: An officer inspects a machine gun team armed with an MG 42 equipped with anti-aircraft sights. The MG 42 was probably the best machine gun of World War II, and had a extremely rapid rate of fire that made it sound like tearing fabric.

the finest weapon of its generation. For squad work it was mounted on a biped and fed by belts or a 75 round saddle drum. Fitted to a Lafette 34 tripod it was capable of accurate and sustained fire at ranges of over 3000 metres. The MG 34 was also commonly used on vehicle mounts, such as the standard armament of infantry-carrying Sd Kfz 251 halftracks, and as an anti-aircraft weapon. It really was an excellent machine-gun, capable of astounding rates of fire, but to quote one small arms expert: 'The design was really too good for military use. It took too long to manufacture and involved too many complex and expensive machining processes. The result was a superb weapon, but actually using it was rather like using a Rolls Royce car for ploughing a field – it was too good for the task.'

■ MG 34
CALIBRE: 7.92mm; WEIGHT (with bipod): 11.5kg (25.35lb); LENGTH: 1.219m (3.7ft); CYCLIC RATE OF FIRE: 800–900rom; FEED: 50 round belts (usually linked together in 5x50 round belt lengths) or 75 round drum

Therefore, the Mauser design team produced a cheaper and simpler weapon, which was even better. The *Maschinengewehr* 42 or MG 42, nicknamed the 'Spandau' by Allied troops, was probably the finest machine-gun of World War II. While it was rugged and well able to stand up to the rigours of service life, what was most extraordinary about the MG 42 was its phenomenal rate of fire of up to 1500 rounds a minute. It could go through a 250 round belt in less than 15 seconds. This was two to three times the rate of most Allied weapons, and the noise of a MG 42 firing has

been compared with that of a bandsaw or tearing linoleum. Such a rate of fire meant that the machine-gun's barrel had to be regularly changed and this could be done in under five seconds. It was distributed widely from the end of 1942 onwards, and meant that panzergrenadiers could put up prodigious amounts of fire in defence.

■ MG 42
CALIBRE: 7.92mm; LENGTH: 1.220m (3.72ft); WEIGHT: 11.5kg (25.36lb); CYCLIC RATE OF FIRE: up to 1500rpm; FEED: 50 round belt

Such was the need for machine-guns that numerous foreign designs were pressed into service. Amongst the best was the Czechoslovak ZB vz 26 and ZB vz 30, known in German service as the MG 26(t) and MG 30(t) respectively, and which formed the basis of the famous British Bren gun. It is a testament to these designs that virtually their entire production went to the Waffen SS.

Flamethrowers

Each panzergrenadier regiment would contain an engineer platoon. In the German army, engineers undertook a variety of tasks but were often in the forefront of combat, particularly when assaulting enemy fortifications. In the attack they used specialist equipment such as shaped explosive charges and flamethrowers. The flamethrower is an especially fearsome device and a useful assault weapon in confined areas. At the start of the war, the standard German man-portable flamethrower was the *Flammenwerfer* 35, which weighed 35.8kg (79lb). Gradually it was replaced by the *Flammenwerfer* 41. Both of these were twin tank weapons: one tank contained the inflammable liquid, the other a compressed gas for propulsion. They were capable of producing multiple short bursts of fire out to ranges of about 30m.

■ Flammenwerfer 35
WEIGHT: 35.8kg (79lb); FUEL CAPACITY: 11.8 litres (2.6gal); RANGE: 25.6 – 30m; DURATION OF FIRE: 10 seconds

ANTI-TANK WEAPONS

Anti-tank rifles

At the start of the war, the principal infantry anti-armour weapon was the anti-tank rifle. Most German infantry companies would be equipped with three such weapons. The standard German anti-tank rifle was the 7.92mm *Panzerbüchse* 39. Originally it fired 7.92mm ammunition with a hard steel core, but examination of captured Polish weapons led to the Germans introducing a tungsten core, which improved penetration. Nonetheless, the anti-tank rifle was rendered increasingly obsolete by heavier tank armour. The single shot rifle could only penetrate 25mm of armour at 300m and thus was unable to tackle any but the lightest tanks or armoured cars after 1940.

■ **PzB 39**
CALIBRE: 7.92mm; WEIGHT: 12.6 kg (27.8lb); LENGTH OVERALL: 1.62mm (4.9ft); ARMOUR PENETRATION: 25mm at 300m

Panzerfaust

The first really effective hand-held anti-tank weapon was the Panzerfaust, which appeared in late 1942. It was a simple tubular projector, which fired a hollow charge grenade and was discarded after use. The first introduced was the Panzerfaust 30, the 30 referring to the 30m range of the weapon. The short range was a considerable tactical disadvantage to the firer, who required steady nerves to achieve a hit, but the Panzerfaust usually proved lethal to any tank when he did. Later models such as the Panzerfaust 60 and the Panzerfaust 100 increased the range (to 60 and 100m respectively). Virtually any Allied tank was vulnerable to this weapon and it was much feared by Allied tank crews. The panzergrenadiers were heavily armed with this weapon, particularly as the war progressed. Most of their vehicles carried at least one stowed away in case of need.

Below: A team of SS panzergrenadiers man an anti-tank gun during the invasion of Russia in 1941. Units were equipped with ever-larger calibres of anti-tank gun as the war progressed, as the size of tanks' armour increased.

■ **Panzerfaust 30**
RANGE: 30m; WEIGHT: Total: 5.2kg (11.5lb); WARHEAD: 3kg (6.6lb); ARMOUR PENETRATION: 200mm

■ **Panzerfaust 60**
RANGE: 60m; WEIGHT: Total: 6.8kg (15lb); WARHEAD: 3kg (6.6lb); ARMOUR PENETRATION: 200mm

In 1943 the Germans captured a number of American M1 bazookas. The Germans quickly produced a much improved rocket launcher, the 8.8cm *Raketenpanzerbüchse* 43. It was an immediate success as an anti-tank weapon and could penetrate 160mm of tank armour at about 150m. It gave off a considerable blast of gas and debris when fired and on the original version the operator had to wear protective clothing. An improved version, the RPzB 54 had a shield to protect the firer. It was operated by two men and panzergrenadiers often carried extra ammunition for the RPzB in special racks on the sides of their Sd Kfz 251 half tracks. The weapon was often nicknamed the *Panzerschreck*.

■ **RPzB 54**
CALIBRE: 88mm; WEIGHT: With Shield: 11kg (24.25lb); ROCKET: 3.5kg (7.7lb); LENGTH: 1.638m (5ft); RANGE: 150m; RATE OF FIRE: 4–5rpm

Anti-tank gun

A panzergrenadier heavy infantry company would usually contain a *Panzerjäger* platoon. This, at the start of the war, would have been equipped with the 37mm PAK 36 anti-tank gun. Although the gun proved successful during the Polish

campaign, later, when it faced more heavily armoured British and French tanks in 1940, the crews often watched in horror as their armour-piercing shells bounced off the enemy tanks. It was also used in the 1941 campaign in the Soviet Union because no larger calibre replacement had been produced in time. The PAK 36 proved utterly hopeless against the T-34.

■ PAK 36
CALIBRE: 37mm; LENGTH: 1.665m (5.07ft); WEIGHT: 328kg (723lb); MAXIMUM RANGE: 7000m; ARMOUR PENETRATION: 38mm at 30 degrees at 365m

The replacement for the PAK 36 was the 5cm PAK 38 which arrived on the front line in 1941. It proved, when equipped with tungsten core ammunition, to be the only gun capable of penetrating the T-34. It remained in service throughout the conflict and was reasonably effective, although by 1945 it had been largely replaced by heavier weapons.

■ PAK 38
CALIBRE: 50mm; LENGTH: 3.187m (9.7ft); WEIGHT: 1000kg (2205lb); MAXIMUM RANGE: 2650m; ARMOUR PENETRATION (tungsten ammunition): 101mm at 740m

The *Panzerjäger* platoons also used the taper bore 2.8cm *schwere Panzerbüchse* 41 (sPzB 41). The calibre of the gun tapered down in size from the breech towards the muzzle and sPzB's special tungsten cored ammunition was 'squeezed' out the barrel at a velocity almost double that of a traditional anti-tank gun. Although a handy weapon given its small size and light weight, the difficulty of production and rarity of tungsten meant that the taper bore system proved something of a blind alley.

■ 2.8cm sPzB 41
STARTING CALIBRE: 28mm; EMERGENT CALIBRE: 20mm; LENGTH: 1.7m (5.18ft); WEIGHT: 223kg (492lb); ARMOUR PENETRATION: 56mm at 365m

The increasing thickness of Soviet tank armour meant that something heavier was needed than the 50mm PAK 38 gun, although it was an adequate anti-tank weapon. Consequently, Rheinmetall-Borsig came up with a new design that was essentially a scaled-up version of the 50mm gun in a larger 75mm calibre. The result was the 7.5cm Pak 40, which, naturally enough, resembled a larger version of its smaller sibling. It was also an excellent gun, capable of dealing with virtually any tank used by the Allies on all fronts. German anti-tank gunners rated it their best weapon, and it was flexible enough in its range of ammunition to make a reasonable artillery piece when firing high explosive shells.

KARABINIER 98K *Calibre:* **7.92mm (0.31in)**; *Length:* **110.7cm (43.6in)**; *Weight (unloaded):* **3.9kg (8.6lb)**; *Magazine* **5-round integral box**; *System of operation:* **bolt action**; *Muzzle velocity:* **755mps**

MG 34 *Calibre:* **7.92mm (0.31in)**; *Length:* **122cm (48in)**; *Weight:* **12.1kg (26.7lb)**; *Feed:* **belt, 50-round drum or 75-round saddle drum**; *System of operattion* **short recoil**; *Rate of fire (cyclic):* **800–900rpm**; *Muzzle velocity:* **756mps**

However, it was a formidable anti-tank weapon. Using tungsten-cored AP40 ammunition (all too rare) it could penetrate 98mm of amour plating at 2000m. At the more typical combat range of 500m this increased to 154mm. The PAK 40 was a gun Allied tank men rightly feared.

■ **PAK 40**
CALIBRE: 75mm; LENGTH: 3.7m (11.3ft); WEIGHT: 1425kg (3142lb); MAXIMUM RANGE: (HE) 7680m; ARMOUR PENETRATION (tungsten ammunition): 98mm at 2000m

INFANTRY SUPPORT WEAPONS

Mortars

Panzergrenadier battalions carried a considerable amount of firepower. Infantry companies would usually have two or three 50mm or 80mm mortars and later Type 44 formations often had a mortar platoon equipped with large 120mm weapons. The Germans made themselves masters in the handling of mortars and were experts at bringing down mortar barrages on Allied positions. During the Normandy campaign, mortars were responsible for an extraordinary proportion of British and American casualties – 75 per cent for much of the campaign. In the first years of the war the standard platoon weapon was the 5cm *leichte Granatwerfer* 36. It was a light overly complex weapon and was phased out in favour of better models later in the war.

■ **leGrW 36**
CALIBRE: 50mm; LENGTHS: barrel: 0.465m (1.42ft); bore: 0.35m (1.06ft); WEIGHT: 14kg (30.9lb); MAXIMUM RANGE: 520m; Projectile WEIGHT: 0.9kg (2lb)

The 8cm *schwere Granatwerfer* 34 or 8 cm sGrW 34 held a fearsome reputation amongst allied troops for its accuracy and its rate of fire. Despite its reputation, it was not a particularly remarkable weapon, rather the training of the German mortar crews made it so effective. It could fire high explosive and smoke bombs and could be mounted for use from Sd Kfz 250/7 half-tracks.

■ **SGrW 34**
CALIBRE: 81.4mm; LENGTHS: barrel: 1.143m (3.48ft); bore: 1.033m (3.15ft); WEIGHT: 56.7kg (125lb); MAXIMUM range: 2400m; PROJECTILE WEIGHT: 3.5kg (7.7lb)

On the Eastern Front, the Germans encountered the 120-HM 38 Soviet mortar. They were so impressed that they made an exact copy, the 12cm *Granatwerfer* 42 (12 cm GrW 42) which was issued to the panzergrenadier battalions' heavy company mortar platoons. It was an excellent weapon, with a high rate of fire and a very heavy high-explosive bomb.

Above: German troops use a light 5cm leGrW36 mortar. The Germans proved particularly adept in their use of mortars in an infantry support role. Mortars gave the Germans a measure of fire support that was not easy to detect or destroy from the air.

■ **12cm GrW 42**
CALIBRE: 120mm; LENGTHS: barrel: 1.862m (5.68ft); bore: 1.536m (4.68ft); WEIGHT: 280.1kg (617.6lb); MAXIMUM RANGE: 6000m; PROJECTILE WEIGHT: 16kg (35.28lb)

Infantry Guns

German tactical doctrine required that each battalion had artillery support available, and it was appreciated that special light guns would suit this role. The standard weapon in this category was the 7.5cm *leichte Infrantriegeschütz* 18 or leIG 18, which entered service in 1932. A panzergrenadier or motorised infantry battalion's heavy company might have one or two two-gun 7.5cm leIG 18 support sections. The gun proved sturdy and reliable, though it had a limited range due to its short barrel. The leIG 18 was supposed to have an anti-tank capability using hollow charge ammunition, but this was ineffective and was little used.

■ **7.5cm leIG 18**
CALIBRE: 75mm; LENGTH OVERALL: 0.9m (2.74ft); WEIGHT: 400kg (882lb); MAXIMUM range: 3550m; PROJECTILE WEIGHT: 5.45 or 6kg (HE) (12 or 13.23lb)

The panzergrenadier support companies also used heavy weapons such as the 15cm *schwere Infantriegeschütz* 33 or sIG 33. It was an orthodox if somewhat heavy weapon. Although ideally it could be mounted on a self-propelled carriage and

Above: An infantry section clustered by a Sdfk 210 halftrack armed with a 2cm Flak 30 anti-aircraft gun await orders whilst on training manoeuvres in France. The man standing is armed with an MP40, whilst his colleagues carry Gewehr 98k rifles.

thus correspond with Guderian's ideas of mobile artillery instantly ready to support the tanks, in reality the sIG 33 was very often towed by truck or tractor. In infantry divisions it was usually horse-drawn. Typical self-propelled mounts were the Sd Kpf 138/1 or the Pz Kpfw I chassis (the only self-propelled artillery available during the French campaign). In this role it proved a powerful support weapon.

■ **15cm sIG 33**
Calibre: 149.1mm; Length: barrel 1.65m (5.03ft); Weight: 1750kg (3859lb); Maximum Range: 4700m; Projectile weight: 38kg (HE) (83.79lb)

Field Artillery and Howitzers
The standard German field howitzer was the 10.5cm *leichte Feldhaubitze* 16 (leFH 16), which equipped the light battalions of a panzergrenadier division's artillery regiment. It was a sound and sturdy piece, with a useful range and weight of shell. It was perhaps rather too sturdy for its purpose, because its considerable weight meant that the 10.5cm leFH could not be dragged out of the all-prevailing mud in Russia when the weather worsened, thereby limiting its effectiveness as a support weapon.

■ **10.5cm leFh 18/40**
Calibre: 105mm; Length: 3.31m (10.08ft); Weight: 1955kg (4311lb); Range: 12,325m; Projectile weight: 14.81kg (32.66lb)

Germany's heavy field howitzer was the 15cm *schwere Feldhaubitze* 18 (sFH 18). This gun equipped the division's heavy artillery battalion. It was a reliable and sound piece, although on the Eastern Front the Germans found that it was outranged by the Soviet 152mm equivalent. As the war went on the sFH 18 was placed on a self-propelled carriage known as the *Hummel* and served as the mobile artillery in a number of panzer and panzergrenadier divisions.

■ **15cm sFH**
Calibre: 149mm; Length: 4.44m (13.4ft); Weight: 5512kg (12,154lb); Maximum range: 13,325m ; Projectile Weight: 43.5kg (95.9lb)

Many panzergrenadier divisions also contained a 10.5cm *Kanone* 18 gun battery. These were far from satisfactory, being much too heavy for the weight of shell fired. Admittedly the 10.5cm K 18 had a very decent range, but it was only in service because other weapons were not available in enough numbers.

■ **10.5 cm K 18**
Calibre: 105mm; Length: 5.46m (16.64ft); Weight: 5624kg (12,401lb); Range: 19,075m; Projectile weight: 15.14 kg (33.38lb)

The heaviest artillery pieces that might equip a panzergrenadier division were the 17cm *Kanone* 18 and the 21cm *Mörsers*. For example, the 15th Panzer Grenadier Division's 33rd Panzer Artillery Battalion had three batteries of the 170mm K 18 and a single battery of the heavier weapon. Despite their considerable size (and weight) both were excellent howitzers, and fired a wide range of useful projectiles in support of the panzergrenadiers.

■ **17cm K 18**
CALIBRE: 172.5mm; LENGTH: 8.529m (28ft); WEIGHT: 17,520kg (38,632lb); MAXIMUM RANGE: 29,600m; PROJECTILE WEIGHT: 68kg (150lb) (HE)

■ **21cm Mörser 18**
CALIBRE: 210.9mm; LENGTH: 6.51m (21.4ft); WEIGHT: 16,700kg (36,817lb); MAXIMUM RANGE: 16,700m; PROJECTILE WEIGHT: 121kg (267lb) (HE)

The demands to equip panzergrenadier divisions with enough artillery led to much captured equipment being used. For example, in September 1943 the 18th Panzer Grenadier Division's 18th Artillery Regiment had a battery of 152mm Russian howitzers in its 1st Battalion and a battery of 155mm French guns in its 3rd Battalion. Such a variety of guns could lead to problems with ammunition supply.

Anti-Aircraft Guns

As noted above, the panzergrenadier division was an all-arms formation. Although the proportion of anti-aircraft guns was small at the start of the war, experience soon taught the Germans to include more and more, and heavier and heavier, anti-aircraft guns in their divisions. While a 1939 motorised infantry division contained only 12 20mm flak guns, by 1944 a panzergrenadier division would have at least 40 20mm, plus a number of 20mm quads, some 37mm guns and, in its heavy anti-aircraft battalion, 8 of the famous 88mm flak guns. As the Allies dominated the skies of Europe, considerable integral anti-aircraft firepower was required by a panzergrenadier division.

A scene from the training manual, illustrating how a line of panzergrenadiers can be staggered, as long as the rearmost man is closer to the two men in front of him than the distance between them, to avoid fatal accidents.

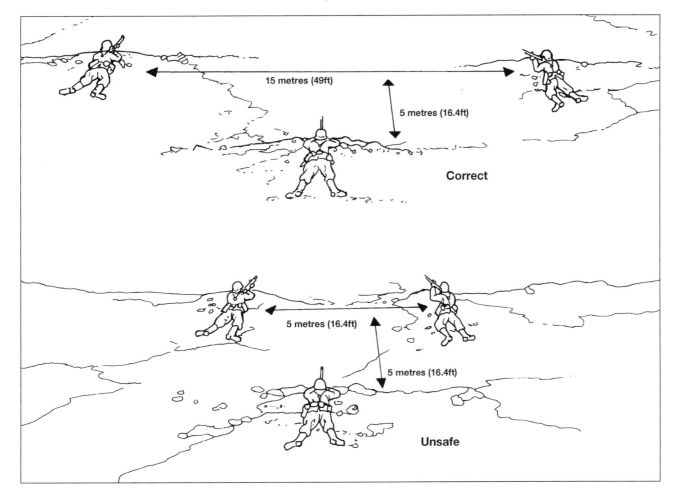

Above: A section of panzergrenadiers form up on the Russian steppe behind a Pz Kpfw III. As the war went against the Germans and tanks grew fewer in number, the panzergrenadiers would frequently advance ahead of the tanks to help protect them.

Although machine-guns also provided local air defence, the lightest-calibre dedicated air defence weapons were of 20mm calibre. The most common German design was the 2cm Flak 38, which could pump out the rounds at 420 to 480 per minute. It could also be used against ground targets. In 1940, to further increase the effectiveness of these weapons, the 2cm *Flakvierling* 38 was developed. This was simply a Flak 38 carriage modified to take four barrels. This combination proved dreadfully effective against low-flying Allied aircraft. These quad 20mm guns were often mounted on vehicles such as Sd Kfz 7/1 halftracks to provide more mobile air defence.

■ **Flak 38**
CALIBRE: 20mm; LENGTH: 2.2525m (6.87ft); WEIGHT: 420kg (926lb); EFFECTIVE CEILING: 2200m (6710ft); RATE OF FIRE: 420–480rpm

The medium calibre anti-aircraft gun used by the German Army was 3.7cm Flak 36. A sound and effective weapon, the Flak 36 was fed by six-round clips and although intended to take on low-flying aircraft could be used against ground targets if necessary. However, it was difficult to produce and Rheinmetall-Borsig introduced the 3.7cm Flak 43,

which, by using stampings and prefabricated parts, could be produced in a quarter of the time of its predecessor. It also had the added advantage of a quicker rate of fire. In an effort to produce a more effective weapon, a twin-barrel version, the 3.7cm *Flakzwilling* was produced. Both versions were extremely potent guns.

■ **Flak 36**
CALIBRE: 37mm; LENGTH: 3.626m (11ft); WEIGHT: 1550kg (3418lb); EFFECTIVE CEILING: 4800m (14,639ft); RATE OF FIRE: 160rpm

■ **Flak 43**
CALIBRE: 37mm; LENGTH: 3.30m (10ft); WEIGHT: 1392kg (3069lb); EFFECTIVE CEILING: 4800m (14,639ft); RATE OF FIRE: 420–480rpm

The heaviest anti-aircraft weapons in the division's arsenal were the guns of the 8.8cm Flak series: the Flak 18, Flak 36 and Flak 37. Quite apart from being excellent flak guns, they were often pressed into service as anti-tank guns, where their high muzzle velocity and heavy projectile made them ideal tank killers. However, the gun was really too high and bulky to be used comfortably in this role, although its range and power mitigated this somewhat, and on the Eastern Front and in North Africa Allied tanks were often destroyed before their guns could reach the German positions.

■ **Flak 18**
CALIBRE: 88mm; WEIGHT: 5150kg (11,356lb); EFFECTIVE CEILING: 8000m (24,400ft)

ARMOURED FIGHTING VEHICLES

At the outbreak of war a motorised infantry division was exactly that: a division that had been given trucks and therefore no longer had rely on the traditional method of 'foot and hoof' for its mobility. However, in the summer of 1942 a number of the motorised infantry divisions were given a battalion of tanks, which greatly increased the division's firepower. This rapidly became standard procedure. When the motorised divisions became panzergrenadier divisions in 1943 they were equipped with a single battalion of tanks or assault guns. In theory this gave the division a strength of 45 tanks or assault guns. The number of tanks dropped as the war went on, and they were replaced steadily by assault guns. Nonetheless, given the severe shortages of equipment a full strength panzergrenadier division might well have more armour than a depleted panzer division.

Elite formations such as the *Grossdeutschland* Panzer Grenadier Division were even stronger. This favoured division had four tank battalions and one assault gun battalion. The Waffen SS 1st, 2nd, 3rd and 5th Panzer Grenadier divisions had one regiment of tanks and one battalion of assault guns, which gave them the armoured strength of a strong panzer division.

Tanks

Although not as common in panzergrenadier formations as they should have been – assault guns like the StuG III were more usual, as tanks were diverted to full panzer divisions as casualty replacements instead – a number of different tank types were employed.

In June 1942 the 103rd Panzer Battalion of 3rd Motorised Infantry Division contained the three standard German tanks of the period: the Pz Kpfws II, III and IV. The lightest of these was the Pz Kpfw II, which was also operated by the 116th Panzer Battalion of the 16th Motorised Division. By mid-1942 the small Pz Kpfw II was largely obsolete as it lacked firepower and decent armour. They were in the process of being phased out and their chassis were often converted to other uses.

■ Pz Kpfw II Ausf F

CREW: 3; WEIGHT: 10,000kg (9.8 tons); LENGTH: 4.64m (14ft); Width: 2.30m (7ft); HEIGHT: 2.02m (6.2ft); ARMOUR: 35mm front, 20mm sides; ARMAMENT: 20mm cannon, 7.92mm MG; POWERPLANT: Maybach 6 cylinder petrol engine – 140hp; PERFORMANCE: SPEED (road): 55 kmh, RANGE (road) 200km

Of much more combat utility was the Pz Kpfw III medium tank. It continued in production until the summer of 1943 and remained an important part of the panzer arm until much later. Both the 3rd Motorised and the 29th Motorised Divisions operated the Pz Kpfw III until they were destroyed in the battles around Stalingrad in late 1942 and early 1943.

Below: A panzergrenadier squad move cautiously through a village on the Voronezh Front in January 1943. They are supported by a Stug III armed with a L/24 short barrelled 7.5cm gun. They were often attached to panzergrenadier units instead of tanks.

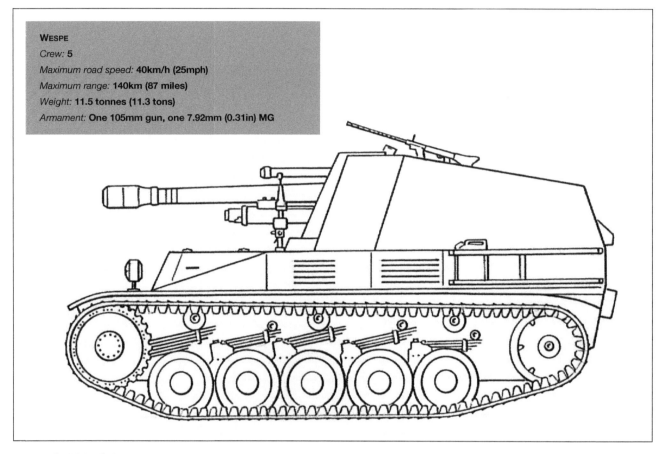

WESPE
Crew: **5**
Maximum road speed: **40km/h (25mph)**
Maximum range: **140km (87 miles)**
Weight: **11.5 tonnes (11.3 tons)**
Armament: **One 105mm gun, one 7.92mm (0.31in) MG**

■ **Pz Kpfw III Ausf M**
CREW: 5; WEIGHT: 22,300kg (22 tons); LENGTH: (including gun)
6.41m (19.5ft), Hull 5.52m (16.8ft); WIDTH: 2.95m (9ft);
HEIGHT: 2.50m (7.6ft); ARMOUR: 50mm front, 20mm sides;
ARMAMENT: 50mm KwK 39 L/60 cannon, 2 x 7.92mm MG;
POWERPLANT: Maybach HL 120 12 cyclinder petrol engine – 140hp;
PERFORMANCE: SPEED (road): 40 kmh, RANGE (road) 175km

The real workhorse of the German panzer forces was the
Pz Kpfw IV, which remained in production throughout
the war and, continually up-gunned and up-armoured,
gave excellent and reliable service in all theatres. The Pz
Kpfw IV was the tank most commonly found equipping
panzergrenadier divisions. It was a match for most Allied
tanks when it was armed with the long-barrelled 75mm
KwK 40 L/48, as most were by the war's end. Despite the
increased strain put on the powerplant by the constant
growth in its armour protection, it retained good mobility.

■ **Pz Kpfw IV Ausf H**
CREW: 5; WEIGHT: 25,000kg (24.6 tons); LENGTH: (including gun)
7.02m (21.4ft), Hull 5.89m (18ft); WIDTH: 3.29m (10ft); HEIGHT:
2.68m (8.2ft); ARMOUR: 70mm front, 30mm sides; ARMAMENT:
75mm KwK 40 L/48 gun, 2 x 7.92mm MG; POWERPLANT: Maybach
HL 120 12 cyclinder petrol engine – 300hp; PERFORMANCE: SPEED
(road): 24 kmh, RANGE (road) 200km

The Pz Kpfw V Panther was the best German tank of the
war. It was arguably the best tank of the war and combined
fearsome firepower, excellent armour protection and
reasonable mobility. The tank, however, was very complex,
which led to mechanical failures and slowed production.
By the end of 1944 the well-equipped *Grossdeutschland*
Panzer Regiment's 1st Battalion contained four companies
of Panthers.

■ **Pz Kpfw V Panther Ausf A**
CREW: 5; WEIGHT: 45,500kg (44.8 tons); LENGTH: (including gun)
8.86m (27ft), Hull 6.88m (21ft); WIDTH: 3.43m (10.5ft); HEIGHT:
3.10m(9.4ft); ARMOUR: 80mm front, 45mm sides; ARMAMENT:
75mm KwK 42 L/70 cannon, 2 x 7.92mm MG; POWERPLANT:
Maybach HL 230 P 30 12 cylinder engine – 700hp; PERFORMANCE:
SPEED (road): 46 kmh, RANGE (road) 177km

Tank Destroyers

The *Panzerjäger* or tank hunter sections of the
panzergrenadier formations, though usually equipped with
conventional anti-tank guns, often used tank destroyers.
These provided the anti-tank sections with considerably
more tactical flexibility and mobility.

The *Jadgpanzer* IV was a tank hunter version of the Pz
Kpfw IV. Its 75mm gun was housed in the superstructure
of the chassis. This provided a low silhouette and the tank

proved popular with *Panzerjäger* troops. In late 1944, the *Jadgpanzer* IV was modified to take a 75mm calibre gun. These vehicles were effective and powerful tank killers.

■ Jadgpanzer IV

CREW: 4; WEIGHT: 2580kg (2.54 tons); LENGTH: 8.58m (26ft); WIDTH: 2.93m (8.9ft); HEIGHT: 1.69m (5.15ft); ARMAMENT: 1 x 75mm PAK 39 gun, 2 x 7.92mm machine guns; POWERPLANT: Maybach HL 120, 12 cylinder engine – 265 hp; PERFORMANCE: SPEED (road): 35kmh, RANGE (road) 214km

The Marder III also saw service. This mounted a 75mm PAK 40/3 anti-tank gun on a Skoda-designed/Czech-built Pz Kpfw 38 (t) chassis.

■ Marder III

CREW: 4; WEIGHT: 1100 kg (1.08 tons); LENGTH: 4.65 m (14ft); WIDTH: 2.35 m (7.1ft); HEIGHT: 2.48 m (7.56ft); ARMAMENT: 7.5mm PAK 40 gun, 1 x 7.92mm machine-gun; POWERPLANT: Praga AC – 150 hp; PERFORMANCE: SPEED (road): 42kmh, RANGE (road) 140km

Assault Gun

Easily the most common and most typical equipment of a panzergrenadier panzer regiment was the *Sturmgeschütz* III. With a low silhouette and reasonable armour, the 75mm cannon-armed StuG III proved itself very useful in battle. Initially it was intended as an infantry support weapon, however, when armed with a longer calibre gun it was also a useful anti-tank weapon.

■ StuG III

CREW: 4; WEIGHT: 23,900kg (23.5 tons); LENGTH: 6.77m (20.6ft); WIDTH: 2.95m (9ft); HEIGHT: 2.16m (6.6ft); ARMAMENT: 75mm gun, 2 x 7.92 mm machine guns; POWERPLANT: 1 Maybach V12 – 265 hp; PERFORMANCE: Speed (road): 40kmh, RANGE (road) 165km

Self-propelled artillery

In Guderian's theory, the perfect panzer formation would contain its own artillery on self-propelled mounts, thus providing rapid and mobile fire support when required by the assaulting panzers. Unfortunately for the Germans, such equipment remained rare; most of the artillery still had to be towed. Nonetheless, a number of self-propelled guns did provide very useful artillery support in some formations.

It was soon clear that the small Pz Kpfw II was obsolete, but as it was in production and quite reliable, it was selected

as a carrier for self-propelled artillery. A 10.5cm leFH 18 howitzer was mounted on the chassis behind an open-topped armoured shield. The result, known as the *Wespe*, proved very successful, with a reputation for reliability and mobility.

■ Wespe

CREW: 5; WEIGHT: 11,000kg (10.8 tons); LENGTH: 4.81m (14.6ft); WIDTH: 2.28m (6.9ft); HEIGHT: 2.3m (7ft); ARMAMENT: 105mm leFH 18 howitzer, 1 x 7.92mm machine-gun; POWERPLANT: 1 Maybach 6 cylinder engine – 140 hp; PERFORMANCE: SPEED (road): 40kmh, RANGE (road) 220km

When it came to mounting a larger howitzer on a self-propelled chassis, the Germans were forced to use a hybrid of the Pz Kpfw III and IV tanks. It used a lengthened Pz Kpfw IV suspension and running gear, combined with the final drive assemblies and track and transmission of a Pz Kpfw III. Mounting a 15cm FH18 field howitzer, the *Hummel* formed the heavy field artillery element of panzer and panzergrenadier divisions from about 1942 onwards, when available. It was probably the best example of German purpose-built self-propelled artillery. Here at last was an artillery piece which could fight at the pace of the Panzers.

■ Hummel

CREW: 5; WEIGHT: 24,000kg (23.6 tons); LENGTH: 7.17m (22ft); WIDTH: 2.87m (8.7ft); HEIGHT: 2.81m (8.6ft); ARMAMENT: 1 x 15cm FH18 howitzer, 1 x 7.92mm MG; POWERPLANT: Maybach V12 engine – 265 hp; PERFORMANCE: SPEED (road): 42kmh, RANGE (road) 215km

Right: A well dug-in battery of 10.5cm leFH(m)-armed Wespe self-propelled guns fire in support of a divisional attack. These were the standard self-propelled guns of a panzergrenadier division for much of the war.

CHAPTER 6

Mobility for the Panzergrenadier

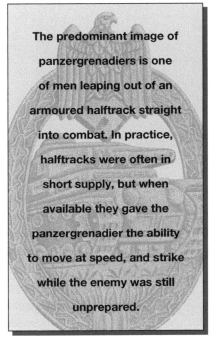

The predominant image of panzergrenadiers is one of men leaping out of an armoured halftrack straight into combat. In practice, halftracks were often in short supply, but when available they gave the panzergrenadier the ability to move at speed, and strike while the enemy was still unprepared.

ONE OF THE PRINCIPAL reasons for the combat effectiveness of German panzergrenadiers displayed during the 1939–45 war was the excellent range of combat vehicles with which they operated. Although the panzergrenadiers co-operated with armour, anti-tank guns and artillery, there was but one chief vehicle with gave the panzergrenadiers the mobility they required to operate effectively on the 1939–45 battlefield: the half-tracked armoured personnel carrier (APC). This new weapon, only invented in the 1930s, forged its combat reputation with the Wehrmacht during World War II, and the engagements fought by these APCs became synonymous with the actions fought by the panzergrenadiers. In the years since 1945, APCs – whether half or fully-tracked – became the chief instrument of today's panzergrenadiers across the world – the mechanised infantry deployed by modern armies.

Origins of the APC

The first armoured troop carriers – prototype APCs – began to emerge during World War I, as did another vehicle which would subsequently influence the genesis of the APC, the armoured car. Typically, these armoured troops carriers were simply modified tanks elongated to carry troops in the

rear hull – the British Army's Mark V Special Tank being a classic example. In the aftermath of the German defeat in 1918, the emasculated *Reichswehr* (German Army) was permitted to retain some 105 dual-purpose armoured cars-cum-troop transporters for internal policing duties. These vehicles provided the Germans with some experience of light armoured vehicles that would stand them in good stead for developing the APC during the 1930s. The other technological experience necessary for the development of the APC was the design of an effective half-tracked chassis: this was provided by foreign expertise.

In the first years of the twentieth century, Adolphe Kegresse, a French engineer, was tasked with looking after the fleet of motor vehicles owned by the Russian Tsar, Nicholas. In an attempt to overcome the problems experienced within this fleet every year due to the extreme icy weather conditions, Kegresse developed a bogie wheel assembly with rubber tracks that he fitted to the rear of one of the Tsar's vehicles to create the world's first half-tracked vehicle. By 1917 the Western Allies had adopted Kegresse's half-tracked vehicle designs and had introduced to the battlefields of Europe the world's first half-tracked armoured cars. The Germans duly responded by copying these Allied vehicles, and in late 1918 introduced the Daimler Marienwagen halftrack to the battlefield, although only four had been completed by the armistice on 11 November 1918. The Marienwagen possessed an Erhardt armoured car superstructure that was simply mounted on top of a Daimler truck chassis that had

---

Left: A section of SS panzergrenadiers seated in their MG34 machine-gun equipped Sd Kfz 251/1 in wintertime. These men are wearing German winter clothing, and the vehicle has been covered in whitewash as a crude camouflage.

Above: In the appalling mud of the Eastern Front, resupply of panzergrenadier and panzer formations proved problematic. Here a
Wiking Division truck becomes bogged down. Many trucks were
converted into halftracks and designated a Maultier (or Mule).

been modified with a simple rubber-band type halftrack
assembly. This use of armoured car design features within a
half-tracked fighting vehicle set a precedent that influenced
the Germans in the mid-1930s when they began to develop
the world's first half-tracked APC.

The APC designs utilised by the German Army during
World War II trace their genesis back to 1926. In that year
the German High Command placed orders for six different
prototype half-tracked troop transporters. Eventually,
subsequent development of these prototypes led to the
manufacture of the range of artillery tractors used by the
Wehrmacht throughout the 1939–45 war. In the second half
of the 1930s further development of the two lightest artillery
tractor designs, including the Demag Sd Kfz 10 vehicle,
ultimately produced the Sd Kfz 250 and 251, the two standard
German half-tracked APCs of the 1939–45 war. The Sd Kfz
250 *leichter Schützenpanzerwagen* (leSPW) light APC carried
just part of an infantry section (six men) into battle, while the
Sd Kfz 251 *mittlerer Schützenpanzerwagen* (mSPW) medium
APC carried an entire ten-man German infantry section into
combat. These two vehicles remained the key weapon of the
panzergrenadiers throughout the entire war.

THE SD KFZ 250 LIGHT APC

In 1939 the German Army designed a lighter APC version
of the recently introduced mSPW Sd Kfz 251, which they
designated the le SPW Sd Kfz 250. This vehicle was based
on the chassis of the Demag Sd Kfz 10 artillery tractor
and featured a scaled-down duplicate of the armoured
superstructure mounted on the Sd Kfz 251. The basic Sd
Kfz 250 halftrack possessed armour some 14.5mm (0.57in)
thick on its front and just 8mm (0.315in) thick on its side
and rear surfaces. Weighing 5.3 tonnes (5.2 tons), the Sd
Kfz 250 could carry a payload up to 1 tonne (0.98 ton).
The rear half-tracked assembly provided the vehicle with
good cross-country mobility, while on roads the vehicle
could reach an impressive speed of 60 kph (37.5 mph). On
each side of the vehicle's rear this assembly comprised five
overlapping wheels plus a slightly separated front wheel;
over all six of these wheels ran the rubber-padded caterpillar
track. At the front of the vehicle was a single set of tyred
wheels. The leSPW entered service with the Wehrmacht
during early spring 1940 and first participated in combat
during the German invasion of the West in May–June
1940. The Sd Kfz 250 possessed a long, shallow hull front,
which ran approximately to the front of the track assembly.
Toward the rear of the vehicle, the superstructure then
rose to form an open-topped fighting compartment with
distinctive sloping sides. Apart from being smaller than the
Sd Kfz 251, the leSPW was distinguishable from its larger
cousin by its fewer tracked wheels (six instead of eight) and
by the fact that its shallow hull bonnet extended further on
the vehicle in relation to its overall length than it did on the
larger mSPW.

Like the Sd Kfz 251, the basic leSPW light APC
normally carried two 7.92mm (0.312in) MG 34 machine
guns to provide close-range offensive and defensive
firepower. These weapons were mounted on pivot devices
at the front and rear of the vehicle's fighting compartment
superstructure. The MG 34 constituted one of World
War II's most effective weapons, and was the world's first
general-purpose dual-role machine-gun. The weapon
possessed an air-cooled barrel which was ventilated by
round holes in the sleeve, rather than the more typical but
cumbersome water-cooling jacket. As a result of this feature
the MG 34 remained relatively light – just 11.6kg (25.4 lbs).
The weapon fired either magazines or 50-round belts at an
incredible rate of 800–900 rpm up to a maximum effective
range of 2000m (2188 yds). Thanks to its twin MG 34 guns,
therefore, the standard Sd Kfz 250/1 troop transporter
possessed sufficient firepower to make close range enemy
infantry action against it extremely hazardous.

Although the Sd Kfz 250 remained less tactically flexible
on the battlefield than its larger cousin, because it could
not transport an entire infantry section, this APC design

nevertheless proved well suited to modification into a range of specialised vehicles. During the course of the war, German firms constructed 14 different versions of the leSPW Sd Kfz 250, some of which duplicated the roles performed by the Sd Kfz 251 variants. Indeed, as even the standard Sd Kfz 250/1 troop carrier – unlike its larger Sd Kfz 251 cousin – could not carry an entire infantry squad, the Germans often used this troop transporter in specialised roles, such as a platoon commander's vehicle. As the war progressed the basic design of the leSPW underwent numerous minor modifications designed to simplify the construction process, and thus increase the rate at which German firms could deliver new vehicles to the battlefield troops. The bolted-on stowage compartments, for example, became incorporated into the basic superstructure design in order to simplify manufacture.

HEAVY WEAPONS SD KFZ 250 VEHICLES

As with its larger sister vehicle the Sd Kfz 251, the Germans manufactured several versions of the leSPW as heavy weapons vehicles, either with cannon or other firepower systems. During 1942–43 – in the middle phase of the war –

the panzergrenadiers on the Eastern Front were clamouring desperately for enhanced anti-armour firepower to resist the threat posed by the Soviets' potent T-34 medium tank. In response, the German High Command decided to develop a series of more heavily-armed variants of the leSPW. Perhaps the most obvious decision by the German procurement agencies was to develop a lighter Sd Kfz 250 version of the already deployed Sd Kfz 251/9 heavy weapons vehicle which mounted the short barrelled 7.5cm KwK L/24 calibre tank gun, which before then had been mounted in the early Panzer IV tank models. This vehicle, the Sd Kfz 250/8, first entered service in mid-1943 to equip some of the six-vehicle heavy gun platoons found within panzergrenadier battalions. In addition to its 7.5cm cannon, the Sd Kfz 250/8 also mounted the newer 7.92mm MG 42 machine-gun above its main armament. The crew used the MG42, firing tracer rounds, as a sighting and ranging instrument for the 7.5cm cannon, although obviously the machine-gun could also be used to deadly effect as a close-range defensive fire weapon against enemy infantrymen.

As the German Army in the east began to face mounting Red Army pressure during 1942–43, it became increasingly obvious to the German High Command that their lightly

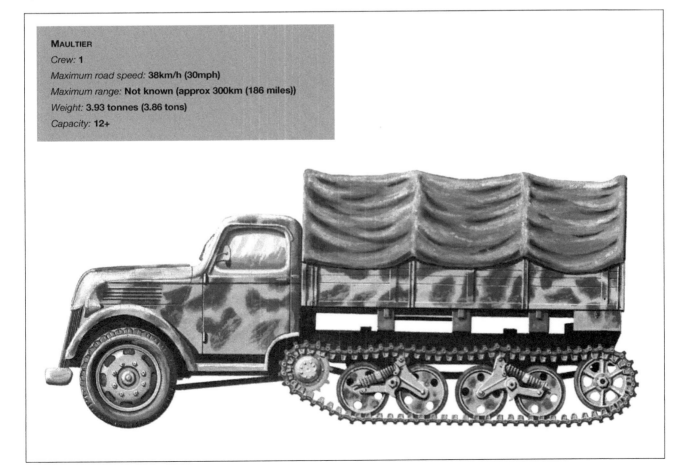

MAULTIER
Crew: **1**
Maximum road speed: **38km/h (30mph)**
Maximum range: **Not known (approx 300km (186 miles))**
Weight: **3.93 tonnes (3.86 tons)**
Capacity: **12+**

armed and lightly protected wheeled armoured cars, like the Sd Kfz 222, were becoming tactically marginalised. In addition, compared with wheeled armoured cars, German half-tracked vehicles proved more manoeuvrable over rough terrain and enjoyed better records of mechanical reliability. To alleviate this situation, the German procurement office decided to develop gun-armed versions of the Sd Kfz 250 light half-tracked APC that could perform the scouting missions formerly undertaken by armoured cars. This model, the Sd Kfz 250/9, entered service in 1943, and was designed to supersede the wheeled Sd Kfz 222 light armoured car within the German order of battle on the Eastern Front. The 250/9 simply mounted the complete, six-faceted, turret of the Sd Kfz 222 armoured car on top of a modified, roofed-in, Sd Kfz 250 APC superstructure.

Anti-tank APC

In this middle period of the war, the heavy companies of German panzergrenadier battalions also began to receive deliveries of another heavy weapons leSPW half-track. This vehicle, the Sd Kfz 250/10, mounted the 3.7cm (1.46in) Pak 36 anti-tank gun in a small, open shield on the upper front edge of the crew's fighting compartment. The 3.7cm Pak 35/36 weapon, first introduced in 1935, became the standard anti-tank gun of the German Army during the early war years. The gun could be mounted on the existing

Sd Kfz 250 (and indeed also the Sd Kfz 251) superstructure because it only weighed 432kg (952.5 lbs). The 42 calibre-long 3.7cm barrel could fire its rounds at a muzzle velocity of 762m/s (2500 ft/s) to a maximum range of 4025m (4400 yds). Effective typical combat ranges were significantly less than this – usually below 800 yards. Although this vehicle provided some additional anti-tank capability for the panzergrenadiers, by 1942 the Pak 35/36 gun was scarcely a match for the increasingly well-protected Soviet armoured vehicles now being encountered on the battlefields of the east, unless the Sd Kfz 250/10 APC closed to engage the enemy at very close range – a risky endeavour for such a lightly-armoured vehicle.

This ever growing front-line demand for increased anti-tank capabilities within German panzergrenadier units also led the German Army in 1942 to introduce yet another heavy weapons version of the leSPW light APC. This vehicle, the Sd Kfz 250/11, mounted the 2.8cm (1.1in) schwere Panzerbüchse 41 (sPzB 41) tapered-bore anti-tank rifle on its superstructure front. The barrel of the sPzB 41 tapered from an initial 2.8cm (1.1in) to an ultimate 2cm (0.788in), squeezing its malleable tungsten round to provide a significantly enhanced muzzle velocity of 1400 m/s (4596 ft/s). Although classified as an anti-tank rifle, the weapon looked like a slightly scaled-down version of a light anti-tank gun. Although the sPzB 41 had proved a useful tank killer during 1942, by the time that numbers of the Sd Kfz 250 had been fitted with this weapon, its tactical impact on the battlefield was rapidly diminishing in the face of the improved levels of armour now sported by Soviet tanks.

Below: A section of infantry debus rapidly from a light Sd Kfz 250 halftrack. Panzergrenadiers would usually exit from the rear of a halftrack, rather than the sides, as leaping over the side of the vehicle left men extremely exposed to enemy fire.

Sd Kfz 250/10
Crew: **6**
Maximum road speed: **59.5km/h (37mph)**
Maximum range: **299km (186 miles)**
Weight: **5380kg (11,861lb)**
Armament: **One 37mm (1.45in) gun**

In addition to the gun-armed heavy weapons vehicles described above, the German Army also deployed one other, non-gun-armed, heavy weapons variant of the leSPW light APC. This vehicle was the Sd Kfz 250/7 mortar carrier, and as the war progressed this vehicle increasingly replaced the larger Sd Kfz 251/1 mortar-firing half-track. The 250/7 carried a 8cm (3.15in) *Granatwerfer* 34 (8cm GW 34) mortar located in the open-topped crew fighting compartment. Although technically the crew could fire the GW 34 from the 250/7 vehicle, in practice on the battlefields of Europe, German crews preferred to set-up the mortar close to the vehicle but in a concealed location, and fire it from there. Surprisingly, despite its designation, the 8cm GW 34 was actually a 81mm (3.2in) calibre weapon.

Command and Control APCs

In addition to these heavy weapons vehicles, German panzergrenadier battalions also deployed a number of command and control versions of the Sd Kfz 250 APC. One such vehicle was the Sd Kfz 250/3 command halftrack which carried powerful radio devices supported by either a distinctive rail or star antennae – the tell-tale identifying feature of all German armoured command vehicles, whether fully-tracked, half-tracked or wheeled. Probably the most famous Sd Kfz 250/3 vehicle was 'Greif' ('Griffin'), Field Marshal Rommel's command APC during the North Africa campaign. The Sd Kfz 250/4 was an almost identical command version of the Sd Kfz 250/3, but designed for use by Luftwaffe ground–air cooperation liaison officers attached to the headquarters companies of German panzergrenadier battalions. Other command and control versions of the leSPW developed included the 250/2 telephone line laying vehicle, and the derivative Sd Kfz 253 *leichte gepanzerte Beobachtungswagen*, a dedicated light armoured observation halftrack.

The last range of leSPW variants utilised by German panzergrenadiers carried out a variety of support and ancillary roles. The Sd Kfz 250/6 *Muntionswagen* featured a cut-back rear superstructure and was designed to carry ammunition to resupply the other vehicles deployed within the panzergrenadier battalion. A similar vehicle, the derivative Sd Kfz 252 *leichte gepanzerte Munitionswagen*, was also fielded within panzergrenadier battalions to carry additional ammunition for the unit's other vehicles. The Sd Kfz 250/12 *leichte Messtrupppanzerwagen* was a highly specialised support vehicle for the survey section attached

Above: A selection of a panzergrenadier reconnaissance vehicles. At the front left is a Sd Kfz 222 2cm cannon-armed armoured car. Behind it is a Sd Kfz 232 radio car and to the right is a heavier *Panzerspahwagen* **Sd Kfz 232 (8rad) communication vehicle.**

to the organic artillery units fielded in each German panzer and panzergrenadier division.

The German Army manufactured sizeable numbers of the 14 variants of the Sd Kfz 250 leSPW light halftrack during World War II, although this was significantly fewer than for the larger Sd Kfz 251 APC. From just a few hundred in late 1940, the numbers of Sd Kfz 250 vehicles in German service rose to some 3500 in 1943, before falling to just 2182 vehicles in November 1944. Consequently, although a seemingly ubiquitous vehicle within German panzer and panzergrenadier divisions, the Sd Kfz 250 was never a common vehicle, and actual numbers in service never reached the theoretical norms.

SD KFZ 251 MEDIUM APC

Although numerically designated after the Sd Kfz 250, the larger, 8.5-tonne (8.3-ton) Sd Kfz 251 medium APC in fact

pre-dated its smaller cousin. As far back as 1935, the German High Command accepted the recently developed 3-tonne (2.95-ton) half-tracked artillery tractor chassis as a suitable chassis to design a medium halftrack APC to transport the motorised infantry of the army's newly created first three panzer (armoured) divisions. The design specifications laid down that these APCs should be able to carry a full standard ten-man German rifle squad, in addition to the vehicle's driver and commander. Developmental prototypes fitted a multi-faceted sloping hull superstructure – similar to that mounted on contemporary German armoured car designs – onto a slightly modified 3-tonne artillery chassis, to form the crew's open-topped fighting compartment at the rear of the vehicle. The track assembly comprised seven pairs of interleaved road wheels, plus an eighth front pair, all covered in a rubber padded caterpillar track; at the front of the vehicle was a pair of tyred road wheels. The eight-wheeled track assembly of the Sd Kfz 251 mSPW distinguished it from the smaller Sd Kfz 250 light APC with its six-wheeled assembly. The crew's fighting compartment was not covered over so that the troops could disembark or 'debus' over the superstructure sides, or alternatively they could exit via the rear doors.

When it was developed in the mid-1930s, the Germans did not envisage using the mSPW as a platform from which the panzergrenadiers would fight – what modern armies would term an armoured infantry fighting vehicle (AIFV). Rather the Wehrmacht intended that the Sd Kfz 251 would merely transport infantry to the edge of the battlefield, where they would debus and enter combat. Consequently, the vehicle was relatively thinly protected, in order to keep down weight. The vehicle needed economy in terms of weight in order to maintain a good level of mobility, both along roads and across country; for Germany's light APCs would have to keep up with the rapid advance of the tanks deployed in the panzer divisions. Hence, the vehicle possessed frontal armour just 14.5mm (0.57in) thick, while its side and rear plates were just 8mm (0.315in) thick. As the tactical role of the Sd Kfz 251 changed during the war, this low level of protection would come to haunt the vehicle.

The First Combat Use

During the German Army's first combat use of these medium APCs – the successful September 1939 invasion of Poland – Sd Kfz 251 vehicles were used merely to transport a section of infantrymen to the edge of the battlefield, where they disembarked to join an engagement before re-embarking after the battle. However, during the Germans' May–June 1940 invasion of France and the Low Countries, half-tracked APCs – with their infantry still embarked – often entered action alongside the panzers, providing useful fire support with the vehicle's machine guns and the infantry's small arms. These vehicles often screened the flanks of the advancing panzer divisions, and even disembarked their infantry in the middle of the battlefield to mop up scattered pockets of dispirited and confused enemy soldiers. During this campaign, given that the poorly-prepared Western Allies could not cope with the high tempo and momentum of German mechanised operations, such tactical use of the Sd Kfz 251 did not turn out to be expensive in terms of casualties.

Given these useful tactical services provided by German APCs in France, during the June 1941 German invasion of the Soviet Union, Operation Barbarossa, the Wehrmacht used these APCs as front-line combat vehicles within the panzer divisions. However, when used in this role during

Below: The motorcycle was a vital mobile component of any German armoured formation. It could act as a reconnaissance vehicle or even a troop carrier, and served on all the fronts during World War II.

the bitter battles that raged on the Eastern Front during 1941–42, the lack of firepower and – especially – the poor level of armour protection possessed by the Sd Kfz 251 became painfully clear. Consequently, the panzergrenadiers experienced rapidly rising casualty rates in combat. Unfortunately, the design offered little scope for increasing the levels of protection afforded to the panzergrenadiers, and this would affect German employment of the mSPW in such a front-line role for the rest of the war: consequently, loss rates of these vehicles remained as high during the last three years of the war as they had been during the Operation Barbarossa campaign.

Despite German attempts to up-gun the Sd Kfz 251, the battles fought during 1943 demonstrated clearly that the lightly armoured mSPW remained far too vulnerable to enemy fire to be used in the midst of battle. However, the growing menace posed by infantry anti-tank weapons like the bazooka compelled the Germans to continue employing the Sd Kfz 251 in the van of the battle. By 1944, these APCs often even pushed forward in front of the armour to neutralise enemy tank destruction squads, by using their machine guns.

By 1945, with the steadily weakening German Army relying on static defences to a greater degree in the face of the inexorable Allied advance, German APC tactics again altered. Reverting to the 1939 model, APCs tended to transport their infantry section to the edge of the battlefield, to man static defences, before the heavy weapons APCs withdrew to provide fire support with their cannon from the rear. The Sd Kfz 251 vehicles lacking cannon would be deployed with small groups of tanks as mobile counter-attack forces.

The Sd Kfz Enters Service

The German Army began field trials of the first Sd Kfz 251 prototypes during 1938, and began general production of the vehicle from 1939. Initially, like most German vehicle production, manufacture of the Sd Kfz 251 commenced at a desultory rate. Consequently, by the start of the war in September 1939, the German Army could field just 69 Sd Kfz 251 half-tracked APCs: the vast majority of the motorised infantry within Germany's six panzer divisions remained lorryborne. Construction of the mSPW continued slowly during 1940, when only 355 were delivered. The limited availability of APCs meant that the Germans authorised

Below: A view of an Sd Kfz 251/1 moving through Russian mud, demonstrating the type's manoeuvrability over difficult terrain. Without such vehicles, the panzergrenadiers lacked the mobility that made them such a potent strike force.

SDKFZ 251/1
Crew: **12**
Maximum road speed: **52.5km/h (32.5mph)**
Maximum range: **300km (186 miles)**
Weight: **7810kg (17,218lb)**
Armament: **Two 7.92mm (0.31in) MGs**

only one of the total of six panzergrenadier battalions fielded within a panzer division, to be equipped with APCs. This panzergrenadier battalion, identified from the other five by the suffix (gep) for *gepanzerte*, had an official war establishment of some 150 Sd Kfz 251 vehicles, usually split between five companies.

As the German war economy began to gear into action after the first set-backs in the Soviet Union, so production of the Sd Kfz 251 increased rapidly during 1943, before peaking in 1944, when some 7780 Sd Kfz 251 vehicles were produced, at a rate of 657 per month. By May 1945 the German Army had received as many as 16,300 of these medium APCs. Despite this burgeoning production, the number of mSPW vehicles operational in a panzer division at any given time remained relatively modest, as the number of mechanised divisions grew and as high battlefield losses made their mark. Even at the time that the strength of Sd Kfz 251 vehicles in German service peaked – some 6155 vehicles on 1 December 1944 – this amounted to approximately 120 units per division, since the Germans now deployed about 50 mechanised formations that fielded APCs (including 30 panzer divisions, 11 panzergrenadier divisions, and seven independent panzer brigades). Elite units, such as the Waffen-SS panzer divisions and the

Wehrmacht's *Grossdeutschland* and *Lehr* Divisions, often fielded between 150 and 200 Sd Kfz 251 vehicles, thus many ordinary German panzer and panzergrenadier divisions may have deployed just 60–80 of these vehicles: almost certainly, a proportion of these vehicles would also have been temporarily non-operational due to mechanical problems, so the number of APCs available at any given moment was even less than these figures suggest.

The increases in the production rates of the mSPW achieved during 1942–44 were accomplished in part by a series of modifications to the vehicle's design intended to simplify and speed the construction process. During the war, four main models of the Sd Kfz 251 emerged. The first two, the Models A and B, emerged during 1939–40. The Model C first entered service during mid-1940 and featured a single section nose plate instead of the earlier two-piece plate, designed to simplify manufacture. In 1942, the Sd Kfz 251 was completely redesigned to produce the Model D. This variant featured large single piece superstructure plates instead of the individual faceted ones possessed by previous versions. This redesign significantly speeded the manufacturing process, and the Model D remained in production without significant modification until the end of the war. Although examples of all four types continued to see service until the end of the war, the majority of the Model D vehicles served with select formations such as the Waffen-SS panzer divisions, or the elite Wehrmacht ones, such as the *Grossdeutschland* Division.

As the war developed, the requirement for the Sd Kfz 251 to fulfil new, specialised, battlefield roles became increasingly apparent to the German High Command, as did the need for enhanced levels of protection and firepower. These two requirements led ultimately to the emergence of no less than a total of 22 variants of the basic Sd Kfz 251 halftrack model over the course of World War II. These variants fall into a series of grouped functional vehicles that include gun-armed heavy weapons vehicles, non-gun-armed heavy weapons vehicles, anti-aircraft APCs, command and control vehicles, and miscellaneous support APCs.

Increased Fire Support

As the bitter Eastern Front battles raged through 1941–42, it became increasingly clear to the German Army that their panzergrenadiers lacked organic direct fire support to deal with the increasingly potent Soviet tank and anti-tank capabilities. The obvious solution was to mount heavier

---

Below: A Sd Kfz 251 demonstrates its 'swimming' capability whilst crossing a river in Poland. Even such a basic amphibious ability as this could save the panzergrenadiers time during an assault or pursuit, and help keep up the pressure on the enemy.

guns on the Sd Kfz 251 APC. The first such vehicle was the Sd Kfz 251/10, which entered service in 1941. This vehicle – like its lighter sister the Sd Kfz 250/10 – mounted the 3.7cm (1.46in) Pak 36 anti-tank gun with its shield directly on the forward superstructure, in order to provide protection for the panzergrenadiers from Soviet armour.

By late 1941, when the 3.7cm (1.46in) Pak 36 began to be fitted in the Sd Kfz 251, its combat effectiveness was becoming marginalised by the increasingly heavy armour possessed by Soviet tanks such as the T34. During 1940–41, to prolong the combat life of the Pak 36, whether the standard gun itself or the modified weapon subsequently mounted on the Sd Kfz 251/10 APC, the Germans developed two new, improved performance rounds for the piece. The German Army introduced the first of these enhanced rounds, the 3.7cm (1.46in) *Panzergrenate* 40 (PzGr 40) tungsten-carbide round, in November 1940. The Pak 36 could, when firing normal rounds, penetrate 48mm (1.9in) of vertical solid armour or 36mm (1.4in) of 30-degree sloped armour at the typical combat range of 500m (547 yds) – increasingly inadequate given the level of armour protection possessed by the newest Soviet tanks. But when the Pak 36 mounted on the Sd Kfz 251/10 fired its PzGr 40 tungsten round, the weapon could penetrate a more impressive 64mm (2.5in) of vertical homogenous armour and 54mm (2.13in) of 30-degree sloped armour at the same typical combat range. However, the effectiveness of the Sd Kfz 251/10 was limited by the fact that tungsten for the PzGr 40 round always remained very scarce: the increasingly effective Allied naval blockade of Nazi-occupied Europe prevented importation of this precious resource – and the Nazi war economy could never produce a fraction of the tungsten demanded by weapons such as the sPzB 41 tapered-bore anti-tank rifle and the PzGr 40 round.

In autumn 1941 the Germans developed an even more effective 3.7cm (1.46in) round, which became available for use in the Sd Kfz 251/10 heavy weapons APC. The 3.7cm (1.46in) *Stielgrenate* 41 (StGr 41) stick bomb consisted of a fin-stabilised egg-shaped explosive anti-tank device that fitted over the muzzle of the gun. When the bomb, a hollow-charge HEAT (High Explosive Anti-Tank) round, hit an enemy vehicle, a cone-shaped explosive charge detonated upon impact and shot forward. In so doing it created a pressure wave of molten

plasma which blasted an extremely small hole through even particularly thick armour plate. The creation of this tiny penetration hole then permitted the StGr 41's main high explosive warhead to pass through the vehicle's armour to explode inside the vehicle, killing or at least severely wounding the crew. The Pak 36 anti-tank gun fired the StGr 41 by using a blank cartridge in the breech – a method that duplicated the manner in which an infantryman's rifle fired a rifle grenade. Though the StGr 41 possessed an unimpressive maximum combat range of just 300m (328 yds), use of this weapon increased the effectiveness of the Pak 36; at 300m the StGr 41 could penetrate an incredible 181mm (7.2in) of enemy armour – sufficient to destroy any tank then in service. Of course, the threat posed by such hollow-charge weapons led both the Axis and Allied militaries to develop spaced layered armour which tended to defuse the cone-jet created on impact by such weapons. Nevertheless, with the StGr 41 stick bomb, the Sd Kfz 251/10 remained a potent short-range anti-tank vehicle until newer and more effective anti-tank guns such as the 7.5cm (2.95in) PaK 40 and personal weapons like the Panzerfaust could reach the battlefield in significant numbers.

Up-gunned Sd Kfz

During 1942 the Germans introduced a second gun-armed version of the Sd Kfz 251 into their order of battle on the

Above: Two SS *Leibstandarte* Adolf Hitler Sd Kfz 251s parked in the streets of Kharkov in March 1943. Although the SS were well-equipped, there was always a shortage of these very useful vehicles, a situation which worsened as the war drew to its close.

Eastern Front. This vehicle, designated the Sd Kfz 251/9, carried the short barrelled 7.5cm (2.95in) KwK 37 L/24 calibre tank gun. The KwK 37 delivered a reasonable high-explosive capability as an infantry support vehicle, although its anti-tank capability was less impressive. By 1942, the weapon was virtually obsolete as the main armament of a battle tank – the new Panzer IV versions carried more potent, long-barrelled, 7.5cm (2.95in) weapons. Consequently, as old Panzer IV tanks underwent conversion into a range of tracked support vehicles, significant numbers of the 7.5cm (2.95in) KwK 37 gun became available for mounting in the Sd Kfz 251/9 APC. From 1942, six of these vehicles served in the cannon company fielded within each panzergrenadier regiment. The vehicle provided valuable organic fire support capability and proved popular with the troops; because of the short, stumpy, dimensions of the KwK 37, the Sd Kfz 251/9 soon became known amongst their crews as the *Stummel* ('the Stump').

Although the Sd Kfz 251/10 provided the panzergrenadiers with some organic anti-tank capabilities, the Pak 36 – even with its improved rounds – scarcely constituted an

Above: Sd Kfz 251s cross the fields of Normandy, accompanied by panzergrenadiers who have not been fortunate enough to secure a ride. The constant threat of air attack from Allied aircraft made the use of the halftracks in broad daylight dangerous.

effective weapon on the Eastern Front battlefields of 1943. The Germans recognised that their panzergrenadiers desperately required an effective organic anti-tank capability, and so in 1944 a final gun-armed heavy weapons variant of the Sd Kfz 251 entered service. The Sd Kfz 251/22 carried the potent 7.5cm (2.95in) Pak 40 anti-tank gun, which was mounted on the vehicle's fighting compartment. By 1944 the Pak 40 had established its reputation as a formidable 'tank buster'. With an impressive muzzle velocity of 775 m/s (2528 f/s) when firing armour piercing shells, and 550 m/s (1800 ft/s) with high explosive rounds, the Pak 40 could penetrate as much as 93mm (3.7in) of 30-degree sloped armour at typical combat ranges – approximately 915m (1000 yds).

The only limitation with mounting this weapon on the Sd Kfz 251 was that, even though the roof of the driving cab had been removed, the weapon possessed only a modest field of traverse. Nonetheless, the conversion of this weapon

for mounting on a half-track proved an effective expedient that considerably boosted the anti-tank capabilities of the panzergrenadiers in the field. The only thing that limited the impact of this vehicle was that it was only delivered in small numbers, although it remained in production right through until early 1945.

One other Sd Kfz 251 variant, the 251/22 *Uhu* (Owl), was not a heavy weapons vehicle in itself, but was designed to work with a particularly heavy weapon – the Panzer V Panther medium tank. During 1944, the Germans began to conduct experiments with specially-equipped Panthers which mounted infra-red sights for night-time combat. The Germans believed that such a battlefield capability could prove highly beneficial given the increasingly devastating power of Allied tactical air forces during daylight. The main problem with the effectiveness of the night-fighting Panther, which was equipped with a 300mm (11.8in) *Uhu* (Owl) infra-red searchlight and a Biwa image converter that translated the infra-red image into perceptible light, was that the searchlight's effective range was just 600m (650 yds), which virtually negated the superb potency of the Panther's 7.5cm (2.95in) L/70 gun at long range. Consequently, in 1944, the Germans mounted a much larger 600mm (23.6in) infra-red searchlight on a Sd Kfz 251 halftrack. Two of these vehicles, designated the Sd Kfz 251/22 *Uhu,* were to operate with a night-fighting Panther by providing longer-range illumination for the Panther's excellent gun. The Germans planned that these three vehicles would form the nucleus of a four-vehicle combat team known as the *Sperber* ('Sparrow-hawk'). The fourth element to be included in the *Sperber* team was a standard Sd Kfz 251 intended to carry a full squad of panzergrenadiers equipped with assault rifles that were to be fitted with the *Vampir* (Vampire) night-sight equipment. During 1944–45, production shortages prevented the introduction of the Vampire assault rifle sight, and limited manufacture of the night-fighting Panther and the Sd Kfz 251/22 *Uhu* illumination half-track to just a handful of vehicles. Although several Sparrowhawk teams did deploy in the last stages of the war, it seems unlikely that they ever functioned in accordance with their designated combat role as a night-fighting force.

OTHER SD KFZ 251 HEAVY WEAPONS VEHICLES

In addition to these gun-armed Sd Kfz 251 vehicles, the heavy weapons companies of panzergrenadier battalions fielded several non-gun-armed heavy weapons APCs, the most common of which were mortar vehicles. German factories

modified a small number of Sd Kfz 251/1 APCs so that they mounted six 28cm/32cm (11-12.6in) *Wurfkörper* rockets. These special Sd Kfz 251/1 variants carried the launcher frames along each side of the vehicle's superstructure, set at an elevation of 45 degrees. To fire, the crew had to turn the entire vehicle until it faced the target, and the rockets could only be fired to a fixed range. Despite these obvious tactical shortcomings, the 'Ground Stuka' – as troops quickly dubbed the vehicle – delivered considerable firepower. Furthermore, the conversion was a relatively simple affair which speeded conversion rates – an important factor as the German war economy increasingly struggled to produce sufficient vehicles to meet the vast wastage of material experienced in the front-line. The crews of these special Sd Kfz 251/1 vehicles, however, had to use these weapons with care: if a foolhardy soldier attempted to fire all six rockets simultaneously – instead of in succession – the back blast generated from a full salvo could severely injure the crew or indeed even overturn the APC! A second mortar vehicle fielded by the heavy weapons companies of panzergrenadier battalions was the Sd Kfz 251/2. In a fashion similar to the smaller Sd Kfz 250/7

Below: A panzergrenadier one-ton Zgkw (sf) armed with a 2cm Flak 38 in the mountains of southern Italy in December 1943. As the war progressed, panzergrenadier units were issued with greater and greater numbers of anti-aircraft guns.

Above: SS *Obergruppenfuhrer* **Walter Krüger reviews Knight's Cross recipients of the** *Das Reich* **division after the Battle of Kharkov. He is using a Pz Kpfw VI Tiger as an impressive saluting platform. In the background is a halftrack anti-aircraft conversion.**

vehicle, the Sd Kfz 251/2 carried the standard 81mm (3.2in) GW 34 mortar inside the APC's fighting compartment. Two Sd Kfz 251/2 mortar carriers were fielded in each heavy weapons platoon within the 183-man strong panzergrenadier company.

A final heavy weapons mSPW variant was the potent Sd Kfz 251/16 *Flammpanzerwagen* flame-throwing APC vehicle. Introduced from 1943 onwards, the 251/16 mounted two 14mm (0.55in) flame projectors which were located toward the rear on each side of the vehicle's top superstructure. To supply these weapons with sufficient fuel, the Sd Kfz 251/16 carried two extra, 700-litre (154 gallon) petrol tanks located at the rear of the passenger compartment, which necessitated the welding up of the vehicle's rear doors. The vehicle could

fire 40 two-second bursts of flame from each projector to a distance of 35m (38 yds) over a field of traverse of some 160 degrees. Enemy infantry greatly feared the approach of this APC variant, with its own particularly unpleasant form of – literally – firepower.

ANTI-AIRCRAFT SD KFZ 251 APCs

During the middle phase of the war, the freedom of action the German Army enjoyed on the battlefield became increasingly threatened by the growing impact of Allied air superiority. To protect the combat power of its panzergrenadier battalions, the Germans developed a series of anti-aircraft (Flak) APCs. The first of these vehicles, the Sd Kfz 251/17, entered front-line service during 1943 and served in the anti-aircraft companies of panzergrenadier battalions for the remainder of the war. The Sd Kfz 251/17 mounted a 2cm (0.8in) Flak 30 or Flak 38 cannon mounted on top of the vehicle's rear fighting compartment.

The Flak 30 cannon, which first entered service in 1939, could fire its 0.12kg (0.26 lb) rounds at a rate of fire of 280rpm. The weapon delivered a muzzle velocity of 899 m/s (2950 ft/s) which fired its rounds out to a maximum vertical range of 2134m (7004 ft). The Flak 38 weapon, first introduced in 1940, possessed both greater range and a superior rate of fire (460rpm) than its predecessor. The crew of the Sd Kfz 251/17 APC could fire either of these weapons from inside the APC. Later in the war, a small number of these vehicles featured modified hinged bulging sides that the crew could lower to improve the gun's restricted field of traverse. Moreover, a handful of the last 251/17 vehicles manufactured in late 1944 featured considerable modifications, the most important of which was that they mounted the 2cm (0.8in) cannon in an enclosed remote-controlled turret. The deployment of the Sd Kfz 251/17 within panzergrenadier battalions from 1943 onwards went some way to reduce the negative impact that Allied airpower increasingly inflicted on panzergrenadier operations. Any sustained German movement would attract the attention of fighter-bombers.

During 1944, in a further attempt to ameliorate the impact that Allied aerial mastery exerted on the battlefield, the Germans introduced another anti-aircraft variant of the mSPW, the Sd Kfz 251/21 *Flakpanzerwagen*. This vehicle mounted three surplus German air force 15mm (0.6in) or 20mm (0.8in) MG 151 machine guns. In theory, these cannon ought to have posed a real threat to Allied aircraft, since each MG 151 was capable of delivering a rate of fire as high as 710rpm. However, the main tactical drawback with this cheap and easy conversion was that the Sd Kfz 251/21 could only carry a very modest amount of ammunition for these guns. The Sd Kfz 251/21 served in the flak companies of German panzergrenadier battalions during the last year of the war.

OTHER SPECIALISED SD KFZ 251 VEHICLES

Another series of Sd Kfz 251 variants that served with German panzergrenadier units were command and control vehicles. One such vehicle was the Sd Kfz 251/6 *Kommandopanzerwagen* command vehicle. Produced only in small numbers, the Sd Kfz 251/6 was a dedicated senior officer's vehicle, designed to be used solely by divisional and corps commanders. Consequently, the vehicle's interior

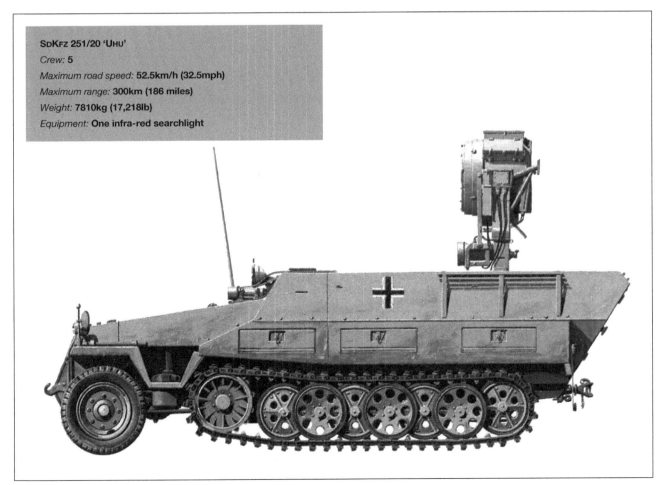

SDKFZ 251/20 'UHU'

Crew: **5**

Maximum road speed: **52.5km/h (32.5mph)**

Maximum range: **300km (186 miles)**

Weight: **7810kg (17,218lb)**

Equipment: **One infra-red searchlight**

Above: Watched by members of the pioneer section of the panzergrenadiers aboard a Sd Kfz 251/7, the rest of the squad clear a fallen tree. A number of pioneer vehicles accompanied the regular panzergrenadiers to deal with such events.

contained office facilities such as enciphering equipment and a fold-down map table. In addition, this vehicle carried several powerful communications systems. Similar APC command variants employed by the panzergrenadiers included the Sd Kfz 251/3 *Funkwagen* radio vehicle, the Sd Kfz 251/11 *Fernsprechwagen* telephone line laying vehicle, and the Sd Kfz 251/19 telephone exchange vehicle.

OTHER SD KFZ 251 SUPPORT VEHICLES

The last series of Sd Kfz 251 variants available to front-line panzergrenadier units was a range of miscellaneous support vehicles. One of these, the Sd Kfz 251/5 *Pioneerpanzerwagen* engineer vehicle, carried small sections of pontoon bridges or assault boats on racks mounted on either side of the vehicle. The Sd Kfz 251/7 pioneer vehicle had increased internal stowage to carry a range of much-needed engineering stores and equipment. The Sd Kfz 251/13, /14 and /15

were specialised sound-ranging and shot-spotting vehicles, designed for use in the artillery units integral to German panzer and panzergrenadier divisions. Other support variants of the mSPW included the Sd Kfz 251/8 armoured field ambulance – often painted with a distinctive red cross on white camouflage background – and the Sd Kfz 251/4 munitions vehicle, designed to carry additional shells for the infantry guns deployed in the gun companies of panzergrenadier battalions.

In whatever guise, the Sd Kfz 250 light and Sd Kfz 251 medium APCs performed sterling service with the German army during the 1939–45 war and represented the key weapon employed by the panzergrenadiers. The APCs gave the panzergrenadiers much greater tactical flexibility and, for part of the war at least, the ability to fight alongside the tanks on the front line.

Much of modern infantry doctrine is based on the tactics that the panzergrenadiers developed in World War II, and many of the infantry fighting vehicles of today can trace their roots back to the Sd Kfz 250 and 251. The impact of these two vehicles on the battlefield of 1939–45 cannot be understated – nor indeed can their impact on military planning after 1945.

WAFFEN-SS OFFICER INSIGNIA

COLLAR PATCHES

SHOULDER

| Colonel General | General | Lieutenant General | Major General | Brigadier | Colonel |

COLLAR PATCHES

Above:
Right-hand collar patch: 2nd Lieutenant to Colonel

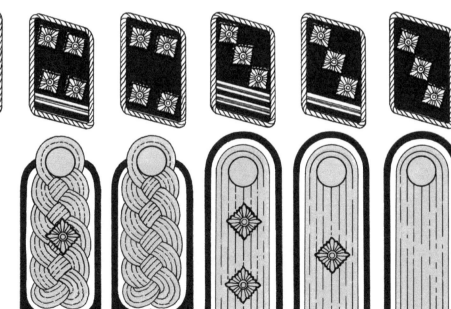

SHOULDER

| Lieutenant Colonel | Major | Captain | Lieutenant | 2nd Lieutenant |

WAFFEN-SS NCO INSIGNIA

COLLAR PATCHES

Above:
Right-hand collar
patch:
NCO ranks

SHOULDER

  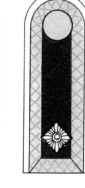 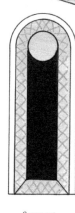 

| Staff Sergeant | Sergeant Major | Senior Sergeant | Sergeant | Corporal |

COLLAR PATCHES

National Insignia:
Left Arm

Colonel General

SHOULDER

 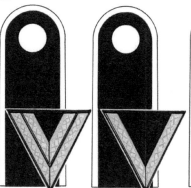 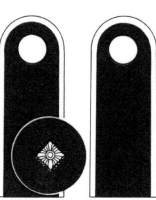

Brigadier

| Senior Lance Corporal | Lance Corporal | Private 1st Class | Private | Camouflage Rank Insignia |

INDEX

References in *italic* indicate captions

aircraft
  Bf109 fighter 38
  Bf110 fighter 38
  Fieseler-Storch Fi 156 34, *34*
  Ju-52 34
  Ju-87 Stuka 33, 37
Aisne *6*
Anschluss 17
Ardennes 33, 34
armoured fighting vehicles 45
armoured personnel carriers *24*, 32, 47,
  77–92
  anti-aircraft 90–91
  anti-tank 80–81
  command and control 81–2
  first combat use 83–4
  lorries replaced by 45–6
  origins 77–8
  Sd Kfz
    222 armoured car *62*
    232 communications vehicle 82
    232 radio car 82
    250 heavy weapons vehicles 79–80
    250 light APC 78–9, *80*
    250/3 'Greif' 81
    250/10 47, 80–81, *81*
    250/11 80–81
    251 7, *15*, 21, *24*, 27, 28, 61, 83, 84–6,
      87, 88
      amphibious ability *86*
      light APC 78–9
    251/1 *77*, *84, 85*
      variants 89–90
    251/2 mortar carriers 90
    251/3 radio vehicle 92
    251/4 munitions vehicle 92
    251/5 engineer vehicle 92
    251/6 command vehicle 91–2
    251/7 pioneer vehicle 92, *92*
    251/8 armoured field ambulance 91
    251/9 *87*
      telephone exchange vehicle 92
    251/10 *21*, *86*
    251/11 telephone laying vehicle 92
    251/16 flame-throwing vehicle 90
    251/17 90–91
    251/21 *Flakpanzerwagen* 91
    251/22 *Uhu* (Owl) 88–9, *91*
  medium APC 82–3

Balletshofer, *Oberleutnant* 55
Battle of Amiens 11
Battle of the Somme 8, 10
Berlin, battle for 58–9
blitzkrieg (lightning war) 7, 16, 32
  tactics *37*
Brandenburg Division 31, 34, 58
British 7th Armoured Division *41*

British troops *10*
  in Normandy 41–3

Caen 40, 42
camouflage *39, 40, 59*
  winter *77*
Canadian infantry, in Normandy 40–41
cavalry 7–8
combat engineers, at crossing of the Meuse
  27–8
command and control
  armoured personnel carriers 81–2
  vehicles 91–2
Courbiere, Second Lieutenant 35, 37

D-Day landings 39
debussing *23, 27*
deployment *65*
Deutschland SS motorised regiment,
  in Poland 33

Eastern Front (1941–45) *23*, 44–59, *57*
Eastern Prussia (1944) *59*
ENIGMA cipher machine *8*
Experimental Mechanised Force 13–14

Falaise Gap 43
Feldherrnhalle Division 24–5
field fortifications 41
firepower *see* weapons
Fourth Panzer Army 55
foxholes 42
France, invasion 25, 33–38
French Army 13, 15
  armoured division 16
Frömmel, Corporal 38
fuel shortages, on the Eastern Front 47
Fuller, Captain J.F.C. 12, 14, 33

Gardki, Lieutenant Colonel Eugen 34
Germania SS motorised regiment,
  in Poland 33
Germany, battle for (1944–45) 57–9
Grossdeutschland Division 24, 25, 31, 33–5,
  37, 48, *61*
  across the Dneiper 49
  at Kursk 55–6, *55*
  officer *33*
gruppe (squad), organisation 27–8
Guderian, Heinz 7, *8*, 10, 15, 17
  Achtung – Panzer! 16, 65
  on armoured warfare 61
  and Kursk 53–4
  and Operation Typhoon 51
  Panzer Leader 14

Haig, General Sir Douglas 10
half-track vehicles 28, *70*
  Daimler *marienwagen* 77
  introduction 77

Maultier *78, 79*
Sdfk 210 *70*
  see also armoured personnel carriers
Harper, Major-General 11
Hastings, Max 39, 43
Hermann Göring Division 31
51st Highland Division 11
Hitler, Adolf 15
Hitler Youth 39
Hoth, Hermann 55

infantry, in Normandy *43*
Inspectorate of Motorised Troops 15
inter-war years 12–17

Kampfgruppe (battle groups) 22
Kampfgruppen Hansen *31*
Kegrese, Adolphe 77
Kesselschlacht (Cauldron Battle) tactic *28*
Knight's Cross 57, *90*
Konig, Captain 35
Krüger, Walter *90*
Kursk *51*
  battle of 52–7
  soviet defences 54–5, 56–7

La Marfée 37
Liddell Hart, Basil 14
losses, in Normandy 43
Ludendorff, General Erich 11, 12, *66*
Luftwaffe 33, 35, 38

mechanical failures 17
Meuse River 33
  battle to cross 34–8
  combat engineers at crossing 37–8
Meyer, Kurt 43
mines, at Kursk 56
mobility 77–92
  lorries 45–6
  M8 armoured car *31*
  motorcycles *13, 17, 27, 47, 83*
  motorised transport 7
  see also armoured personnel carriers;
    tanks
Model, Walter 55
Moscow, advance on 46–52
motorisation, of panzergrenadiers 45–6
motorised divisions, structure 20–21
motorised infantry 16–17, *19*, 20
  divisions 22–4
  renaming 23
  value in Soviet Union 47
  versus panzergrenadiers 32
motorised units *13*

Nacker, Wilhelm 29
Natzmer, von 15
Ninth Army 55
Normandy, battle for 38–43

Offord, Major Eric 14
Operation
  Barbarossa 20–22
  Niwi 34
  Typhoon 46, 49
  Zitadelle (Citadelle) *24*, 52–7, *52*, 53, *53*
Oradour-sur-Glane 47
organisation 19–25
origins and development 7–17

7th Panzer Division 35
panzer divisions, and Operation Barbarossa 21
18th Panzer Grenadier Division 59
20th Panzer Grenadier Division 59
25th Panzer Grenadier Division 59
Panzer Lehr Division 31
III *Panzer-Fusilier* regiment *GD* 56
panzergrenadier
  imprecision of term 32
  origin of term 19, 21
panzergrenadier divisions 22–4, 26
Pirner, Captain 15
Poland, invasion 19, 20, 32–3
Potsdamer Platz 59
pulk (tank and truck formation) 29

river crossings *36*, *37*
Röger, *Unteroffizier* 57
Rommel, Field Marshal 81
Royal Tanks Corps 13–14

Schaaf, Rudolf 39
Schlieffen, General Alfred Graf von 7, 8
Schmeisser, Louis 64
1st *Schützen* Brigade 19–20
Schützen regiments, renamed
  panzergrenadier regiments 21
Sedan 35
Seekt, General Hans von 15, 31
Seelow Heights, battle for 57–8
Signal, German Armed Forces magazine 21–2
Soviet High Command (Stavka) 55
Soviet Union 15, 16, 45
  invasion 20–22, 27
Sperber (Sparrow-hawk) combat team 89
SS
  1st SS *Leibstandarte Adolf Hitler*
    Division 31, 39, *87*
    in Poland 33
  2nd SS *Das Reich* Division 31, 49
    and Operation Typhoon 46–7
  12th SS *Hitler Jugend* Division 31, 39–43
    in Normandy 39–40
    organisation and training 39
    atrocities 47
    reconnaissance troops 46
SS Panzer Grenadier Division *Nordland* 59
SS *Polizei* Division 59
Stalin, Josef 45
Stalingrad, battle 52
stormtroopers *6*, 11
Stummel (Sd Kfz 251/9) 87
Swinton, Colonel E.D. 10

tactics 25–9
tank destroyers
  Jagdpanzer IV 74, 75
  Marder III 75
tanks 7, 73–4
  A7V 11
  Char B1 *bis* 13
  inter-war years 12–15
  introduction 10–12
  Mark 1 Male *10*
  Mark V special tank 77
  and Operation *Zitadelle* 53
  Panzer *see* Pz Kpfw
  Pz Kpfw
    38 (t) *35*, *38*
    I *14*, 15
    II Ausf F 73
    III *17*, *23*, *24*, *47*, *49*, *72*
      Ausf M 74
    IV 23
      Ausf D *48*
    IV Ausf H 74
    V Panther 48, 88
      Ausf A 74
      mechanical problems 54
    VI Tiger 48, *90*
  Somua S35 13
  T-34 48, 54, 58, 86
  vulnerability 25
Thiess, Major General 21
transport *see* mobility
trench warfare 8
Type 44 panzergrenadier division 24–5
Type 45 panzer division 22

uniform *20*, *51*
United States Army 13

Vampir (Vampire) night-sight equipment 89
Versailles Treaty 15
Villers-Bocage *41*

Waffen SS *45*
  NCO insignia 94
  officer insignia 93
  panzergrenadier divisions 25
weapons 21–2, 23–4, 60–75
  anti-aircraft guns *32*
    Flak 18 72
    Flak 30 *70*, 91
    Flak 36 72
    Flak 38 72, *89*
    Flak 43 72
  anti-tank guns 67–9, *67*
    ammunition
      HEAT (High Explosive Anti-Tank)
        round 86
      PzGr 40 rounds 86
      StGr 41 stick bomb 86–7
    KwK L/24 87
    PAK 35/36 80
    PAK 36 68, 86, 87

PAK 38 68
    PAK 40 68, 69, 88
    PIAT 41
    2.3cm sPzB41 68
    anti-tank rifles 66–7
      PzB 39 67
  assault gun
    StuG III *22*, *54*, *73*, 75
      Ausf G *56*
  field artillery and howitzers 70–71
    17cm K 18 71
    10.5cm K 18 70–71
    10.5cm leFh 18/40 70
    21cm Mörser 18 71
    15cm sFH 70
    Soviet 150mm howitzer 57
  flamethrowers *61*
    Flammenwerfer 35 66
  infantry guns 69–70
    7.5cm leIG 18 69
    15 cm sIG 33 70
  machine guns 65–6
    MG 08/15 *6*
    MG 34 65, 66, *68*
      ammunition *29*
    MG 42 66, *66*
    MG 151 91
  Molotov cocktails 25, 58
  mortars 69, *69*
    12cm GrW 42 69
    leGrW 36 69
    mortar crew *21*
    SGrW 34 69, 90
  panzerfaust
    Panzerfaust 30 67
    Panzerfaust 60 67
  pistols 61–3
    Mauser c/96 'Broomhandle' 63
    Pistole P08 (Luger) 62–3
    Walther P38 62, 63
  rifles 63–5
    Gewehr 43 64
    Gewehr 96k *70*
    Gewehr 98k *20*, 63
    Karabiner 98K *39*, 63, *68*
    StG 4464 65
  rocket launchers, RPzB 54 67
  rockets, Katyusha rockets 57
  self-propelled artillery
    Hummel 75
    Wespe 74, 75, *75*
  submachine-guns 63
    MP 40 *25*, *45*, 63, *70*
    PPSh-41 63
  see also tanks
West (1939–45) 31–43
winter conditions, on the Eastern Front 49–52, *50*
World War I 7–12

Zhukov, Marshal Georgi 51

#0030 - 230118 - C0 - 285/213/6 - PB - 9781782745990